MW00778330

An Invitation to

CONTEMPLATIVE LEADERSHIP

How to Lead Mindfully
During Times of Crisis and Uncertainty

THULANI DEMARSAY

An Invitation to Contemplative Leadership

First Edition

ISBN 978-1-914447-53-2

Cover and Book Design: Alexandra Creamer
Author Photo: Stefanie Lynn Photography

Printed in the United States of America
Published by TGH International Ltd.
London, England

www.TGHBooks.com

ABOUT THE COVER DESIGN

As one of the first winged insects to evolve some 300 million years ago, the dragonfly symbolizes self-realization, change, transformation, and adaptability. In many cultures around the world, this unique insect also represents resilience, courage, and one's ability to triumph amidst hardship. Because a dragonfly only flies for a fraction of its life, they are good reminders of the concept of living from moment to moment.

FOREWORD

In June 2010, I had the privilege of participating in a national meeting of 27 contemplative leaders from religious and spiritual traditions, as well as from secular arenas of business, law, leadership, social and environmental justice, education, healthcare, trauma-healing, and end-of-life care. The meeting was co-hosted by the Center for Contemplative Mind in Society and the Fetzer Institute to discuss the state of contemplative practice in America. In preparation for the meeting, each participant was asked to prepare a paper describing contemplative practice, as well as key trends, challenges and opportunities, and reflections on the emergence of a contemplative movement in America from the tradition or arena s/he was representing.

The meeting of contemplative leaders was significant, not because of any grand plan that emerged, but because of what we learned from one another's writing, collective inquiry and experiences of one another's contemplative practice, meditation, and prayer shared at intervals. Over 4 days, we considered the role of contemplative practice—not just for individuals and for the represented traditions and sectors—but also for the cultivation of a society transformed by contemplative values such as peace, compassion, love, justice, forgiveness, gratitude, joy. The papers that each of us had written for one another were later adapted and compiled into a book, *Contemplative Nation: How Ancient Practices Are Changing the Way We Live*, edited by Mirabai Bush. It was, in fact, this book and the paper I wrote for the event, "Contemplative Leadership in Organizations," that provided the first introduction for Thulani DeMarsay and me.

I share about this national event to illustrate how interest in contemplative practice and contemplative leadership has continued to grow and refine itself over the past decade and longer. Thulani is one of five people that I have personally interacted with who have devoted their doctoral dissertation to some aspect of contemplative leadership. The intermingling of practitioners, educators, scholars, and researchers is indeed helping to mature the field, and it is supporting individuals and collective initiatives to reimagine leadership and create social change.

In 2014, the first *Mindful Leadership Conference* was held in Washington, DC with over 500 people in attendance. The following year, The Academy for Contemplative and Ethical Leadership hosted by the Mind and Life Institute was held to "seed a new field of inquiry, practice, study, and research to advance understanding of the role of contemplative practices and mindfulness in leadership for our time." We are living in times of great disruption and unprecedented social and ecological change. Many hunger for leadership marked by "consciousness, conscience, and the capacity to catalyze and influence the larger systemic changes now needed."

In the pages you are about to read, Thulani DeMarsay provides her own evidence of the growth of contemplative leadership in America. She describes how contemplative practices not only impact the leadership of individuals to help one lead from a grounded Inner Self, but also impact the work of teams and organizations to lead from a place of deeper knowing, being, and wisdom in the midst of crisis and uncertainty. She will invite you to stretch beyond where you are presently to find your own contemplative practices and to envision new possibilities for reimagining the field of leadership. There is an urgent need to do so during these times of upheaval.

On a more personal note, in working with Thulani, I knew very quickly that I had met someone with courage and heart, as well as a keen mind. She draws from her experience as a leader and coach, as well as a contemplative practitioner and scholar. The integration is vital for what she has to say about contemplative leadership. There's a big difference between just providing information through another leadership theory, allowing the process of leadership to be personally transformative even as it seeks to transform.

In the course of completing her writing, Thulani experienced unexpected challenges and setbacks. I listened as she described how she used her contemplative practices to access what was deepest and truest within her and make intentional choices about how to move forward. In doing so, she exemplified for me the presence, courage, and integrity to keep "showing up." She didn't choose the circumstances; all she could do was choose how she would respond. Isn't this what most leaders are facing right now, dealing with unexpected challenges and setbacks that most often aren't chosen? But a leader has choices about how to show up, the quality of their presence, and how they will respond (vs. react). The capacity to access one's inner life of leadership makes all the difference to others on the team and in the organization to lean in, listen well, and open up new pathways forward in collaboration with others.

Though Thulani and I have not known one another long, I deeply respect the integrity and congruity that I observed in our time of working together. As you read the following chapters, you will find in Thulani someone who seeks to live authentically what she writes about and coaches others in. Enjoy what you are about to explore, not just with your mind, but with a full-hearted and embodied response to the invitation being offered. Discover aspects of your own true and essential Self through Thulani's Invitation to Contemplative Leadership.

Janet Drey
Managing Director
Consortium for Contemplative Leadership
June 13, 2022

ACKNOWLEDGMENT

I wish to acknowledge with deep gratitude my beloved coach, Michael Torres, for our many conversations about my book, for accepting the invitation to vision, and for holding space during the challenging periods I faced while writing this book. I am eternally grateful to my writing mentor, Karen Mills-Alston, who encouraged me to trust my voice, provided invaluable feedback, and believed that something was truly seeking to emerge from me. Throughout this process, my publisher TGH International took me by the hand and guided me through my first editorial journey. As it did so, I came to admire how it builds a community with its authors and stays true to its mission of being a beneficial presence on the planet.

I hold a deep appreciation for my former dissertation chair, Jean-Pierre Isbouts, who inspired me to transform my dissertation into this book. A heartfelt appreciation goes to Janet Drey for her wise counsel, nurturing spirit, and for gently nudging me to say more. A special thank you to Jonathan Kroll for his support throughout this writing process.

I wish to acknowledge Kristen Sears-Cudd for her editorial gifts and for being a sounding board. My deep appreciation for Kate Teves for her keen editorial insights, thoughtfulness, and for rolling up her sleeves and helping me to finalize my manuscript on time. I owe a debt of gratitude to my dear friend and graphic designer, Alexandra Creamer, for the many hours we spent together on my design and for her meticulous work.

I am forever grateful to my beloved family and dearest friends and mentors for their unconditional love and for supporting me through all my adventures. I am truly grateful to the contemplative leaders I interviewed and spent time with while writing this book. Their insights added depth and richness to this content.

To all of the leaders I've had the opportunity to work with, to learn from, and be led by: thank you for being the inspiration and foundation for this book. I am humbled and grateful for the opportunity to add my voice to this emergent intersection of leadership and contemplative practice.

TABLE OF CONTENTS

"Between stimulus and response, there is a space. In that space is our power to choose our response. In our response lies our growth and our freedom." – Viktor Frankl

Introduction:

An Invitation to Contemplative Leadership

I frequently reference Austrian psychologist Viktor Frankl in my consultancies with leaders and teams. While imprisoned at Auschwitz, he was stripped of everything: his loved ones, health, jobs, possessions, and even his name. In his famous post-war memoir Man's Search for Meaning, he describes that there was one thing he retained ownership of: his inner dialogue. Through all his suffering, he chose his reaction to every given emotion or circumstance.

The above quote of Frankl's reflects his inspiring will to choose. He was an embodiment of resilience amidst crisis and profound uncertainty.

Chances are you are not living under the constant threat of death or annihilation, but perhaps you are facing your own personal struggles and are feeling pulled in many directions. Maybe you are feeling overwhelmed, stressed, or fatigued; maybe as a leader you are burning out. This book is dedicated to Frankl's powerful belief that we can choose how to respond to life's circumstances, regardless of how challenging they may be.

Whether you are a senior leader responsible for running a complex company, an executive director charged with stewarding a non-profit organization, or a millennial entrepreneur who wants to lead more calmly, you have come to this book because something within you resonates with the idea of leading from a place of mindfulness and inner wisdom. On some level, you know that you cannot afford to make decisions with a distracted mind and that you can no longer use all your energy reacting instead of responding. Something within you is calling upon you to listen intently, to hear your heartbeat and to listen to where it is leading you, to pay closer attention, to notice, and to lead with insight. Whatever draws you to this book, I am glad you are here, and I trust you will find what you need within these pages.

For the past 20 years, I have consulted with senior leaders and teams to build resilience and organizational effectiveness. I have worked with a diverse range of leaders, including c-suite leaders, entrepreneurs, and professional men and women. I approach my work through the lens of contemplative practice—a mindful approach that prioritizes a leader's inner qualities and meaningfully cultivates the resilience needed to remain effective under any circumstance. It is an approach that I look forward to sharing with you here.

FROM REACTION TO RESPONSE

In 2019, I was a doctoral candidate at Fielding Graduate University. I was nearing the end of my research, which explored the lived experience of contemplative leaders. I had spent a year interviewing contemplative leaders across the United States, seeking to understand how they were using their reflective practices to foster resilience. Again and again, I encountered inspiring stories of people using centering practices—from meditation to long-distance running to silence—in order to reduce stress, to build capacity, and to lead with grace.

I was close to completing my work when COVID-19 thrust the world into chaos. In March 2020, hospitalizations, deaths, and economic and social disruption tore apart the human family. Many organizations around the world were suddenly in crisis.

The leaders I interviewed during a relatively calm period were now finding their personal and professional contemplative practices put to the test. They were pushed to the edge of uncertainty, and they needed to pivot—quickly—in order to guide their respective organizations through the coronavirus outbreak.

In the coming months, I followed up with each of them to find out how they were doing. Despite the inconceivable challenges, they appeared to be leading with admirable calmness and steadiness of mind. One participant, who led a non-profit of 500 employees, told me that her thirty-plus years of practicing mindfulness meditation and yoga "prepared her for times like these." She also practiced mindfulness while running, which became a tremendous support during the pandemic. Another participant, who is the CEO of a multi-billion-dollar manufacturing company, evoked the Tree of Souls idea depicted in the movie *Avatar*. In the movie, the tree resembles a willow tree and is considered by the Na'vi people to be the closest connection to Eywa ("The Guiding Force"). He compared his contemplative practice to this "guiding force" and stated that there is a "deeper knowing and being" that arises from his personal connection to this source. This connection was helping to keep him anchored through our turbulent times. Finally, I was deeply touched by one of my research participants, a CEO of a firm in New York City, whose father contracted COVID and passed away. Amidst her grief from this personal loss, she leaned in and became of service to others in New York who had lost loved ones. She spoke of how COVID impacted her and the importance of staying in the moment, and she shared how she was honoring the fullness of being human.

Nearly all of the leaders in my study expressed more concern and compassion for their employees than they did for themselves. They cared deeply about how their teams were being impacted, and they were taking practical steps to safeguard their organizations.

These study participants modeled how contemplatively-oriented leaders can flourish amidst chaos and adversity. They demonstrated how meditative and quieting practices can expand a leader's capacity for inner strength, flexibility, resilience, and awareness—how these practices can help them to function calmly and make decisions that benefit both their organization and the humans that make up that organization. I was deeply moved by these leaders' commitment to their respective practices, and their grace became the inspiration for this book.

The pandemic is one of many crises that leaders are facing today. Environmental, security, and political threats all feel, all at once, as if they are more extreme than ever before. This endless array of challenges has steadily chipped away at our resilience, and we find ourselves feeling every day as if "anything can happen." Leaders must prepare now to ensure the sustainability of their organizations in an ever-changing landscape.

While the changes in our world are, on so many levels, frightening, they also present a special opportunity to open ourselves to new ways of leadership. If, as it seems, nothing will ever be the same again, then we have a chance to effect something quite new. This book is about effecting that change—bravely and gracefully.

THE INNER LIFE OF THE LEADER

What makes a good leader? Head into any bookstore and you'll see plenty of authors claiming to have discovered some new, previously unrecognized quality of leadership. But twenty-five hundred years ago, the founder of Taoism, Lao Tzu, may have articulated the most important internal mechanism that leaders must possess in order to remain resilient, effective, and productive, regardless of external circumstances and uncertainty. Writer and Taoist John Heider paraphrased Lao Tzu as follows:

> The leader who is centered and grounded can work with erratic people and critical group situations without harm. Being centered means having the ability to recover one's balance, even in the midst of action. A centered person is not subject to passing whims of sudden excitements...Being grounded means being down-to-earth, having gravity or weight. I know where I stand, and I know what I stand for: that is ground. The centered and grounded leader has stability and a sense of self. One who is not stable can easily get carried away by the intensity of leadership and make mistakes of judgment or even become ill.[1]

---

[1] John Heider (2005). The Tao of Leadership: Lao Tzu's Tao Te Ching Adapted for a New Age. Palm Beach: Green Dragon Publishing.

Think about what this groundedness means to you. Most likely it's a feeling you've experienced at some point in your life, deep in your heart. And yet, if you're like most people, you know that it becomes very, very difficult to access this feeling during times of stress. Perhaps you find yourself feeling adrift, lost, confused, bewildered, overwhelmed, and betwixt-and-between, and no matter how much you tell yourself to "calm down!" you just can't find a way.

This is where contemplative leadership can help.

THE EVOLUTION OF THIS BOOK

My career as a leadership coach has dovetailed with my personal interest in Buddhism. Throughout my study of Buddhism, I have been repeatedly drawn to the concept of "the beginner's mind." This concept refers to the lifelong process of releasing preconceived ideas and approaching life from an attitude of openness, enthusiasm, and humility. Mindfulness pioneer Dr. Jon Kabat-Zinn refers to this experience as an "open attention, moment to moment awareness while seeing things as novel and without judgment."

These qualities are cornerstones of contemplative practices that have served me in my work with leaders and, likewise, with their organizations. Like the leaders I invite to the table of contemplation, my personal practice is intimately connected to my inner self and, thus, to every aspect of my life. It makes sense, then, that I would approach this book from a contemplative perspective and ask readers to engage with it contemplatively. In writing this book, I undertook daily meditation sittings that helped me quietly access my own inner self. Additionally, I engaged in a reflective and inquiry-based process called Life Visioning™ (*covered more extensively in Chapter 6*).

During my research, I embarked on several silent retreats. To be fully present with writing this book, I decided to pack up my place outside of Boston and move temporarily to Southern California. I put work obligations on hold to create the time and space to write and reflect. Free of distractions, I awoke each morning to a panoramic view of mountains and a freshwater lake, the beauty and serenity of which supported my writing.

However, I soon faced an unexpected upheaval that rocked my core and challenged my resilience. My dearest childhood friend, Dia, was diagnosed with pancreatic cancer. So, I returned to Boston to help care for her, and, a couple of months later, she made her transition. The grief shattered my desire to write, but I continued to journal if only for a few moments each day.

That daily practice led to its own revelations.

Through my journaling, it occurred to me that Dia embodied many of the qualities of a contemplative leader. Even as the cancer progressed, she maintained a quiet strength and communicated a sense of inner peace and balance. Dia turned inward, drawing composure from daily meditations, inspirational music, journaling, and reading. Her team of friends and caregivers were all struggling for meaning during this time—each of us was trying to do the best for Dia's care and to stay steady and strong during such a terrible time. Dia led us. Her positive attitude and spirit inspired all in her company as we supported her transition.

Not long after Dia passed, another girlfriend succumbed to Covid-19. Before I could wrap my mind around that loss, one of my beloved coaching clients died suddenly.

There were moments when I considered not completing this book. How could I write while feeling such crushing grief and loss? As a leader, I was facing my own personal crisis. I made a choice to lean in even more on my personal practice for steadiness, inner strength, clarity, and the confidence to continue writing.

During this period, I reflected on the stories of my research participants and what many of them experienced during the pandemic. As I contemplated their struggles and their graceful engagement with their own spiritual and emotional growth, I felt inspired in my practice more than ever. These extraordinary leaders were teaching me exactly what I needed to learn.

I believe that one of the most debilitating suppositions of American professionalism is the notion that reflective experience lies outside the purview of professionalism. Contemplative practices take an entirely different approach to our professional lives. Rather than compartmentalizing and bypassing life's most challenging feelings, contemplative practices invite leaders to lean in, feel, and notice. The hardest experiences in our lives can also be the most illuminating.

It is my honor to present this book, which represents my vision for the future of contemplative leaders. This book offers, as its ultimate goal, a deeper understanding of how contemplatively-oriented leadership can be practically applied within any organizational setting. I hope it provides you tools and practices to lead with greater resilience, focus, and calm.

Each chapter closes with a simple exercise intended to foster reflection and integration. You can find these exercises and more resources to support your contemplative practice on my website, www.thulani.com.

Let's begin.

"Mindful leadership entails being aware of one's internal compass. It enables a leader to respond to a situation as it arises, to respond to the reality of constant changes from a place of deep calm and focus, and to have the presence of mind to face the reality of any situation." – Maria Gonzalez

CHAPTER 1

Leading in the Crucible of Change

The past several years have thrown our country into chaos. The pandemic continues to affect us in far more ways than anyone could have anticipated. As the death toll rises, supply chains have disintegrated, the social fabric has frayed, and an unending series of viral strains have left people reeling. As if that is not enough, a racial reckoning, long in the making, has risen to the surface of our collective consciousness, leaving people compelled to cry, scream, and act.

Meanwhile, the threat of global warming, the divisiveness of social media, the growing absurdity of the political spectrum, and the rising cost of living have Americans feeling like they just cannot catch a break. Just when we thought we might be able to put the challenges of 2021 behind us, the possibility of global war was unleashed on all of us. In fact, in 2022, an annual stress poll by the American Psychological Association indicated that

Americans were more stressed about rising inflation and the war in Ukraine than any other stressors in fifteen years.[2]

It feels as though the future is always hanging by a thread. As the levels of stress mount, we use more and more alcohol, medications, anger, material consumption, and risky behavior to try to keep them at bay, but as soon as one stress is placated, another rises up.

All this pressure does not just stay on the pillow at night. It spills into our work lives and our social lives, impacting our entire society. Short tempers, road rage, and gun violence leave us in a constant state of vigilance as if we are all waiting for something to happen.

During these tense times, it is no wonder that reactive leadership is our default. We long for easy reactions that burn with the same intensity we feel inside. But reactive leadership does not offer lasting, organic solutions for the future. Instead, it expects its practitioners to plow their way through obstacles, no matter the cost to colleagues, to competitors, or to themselves. With this style of leadership, winning is a zero-sum game: you either get what you want or you don't.

It is not difficult to see that this approach will lead inevitably to conflict. Instead of reducing stress for the leader (and for the team, for the community, for the planet), it will only increase it.

If you're like most leaders in our culture, you've probably been employing some degree of reactive leadership, only to find yourself getting nowhere—or worse, going backward. You're not alone in recognizing that the old model isn't working. Hundreds

[2] American Psychological Association, "Stress in America." https://www.apa.org/news/press/releases/stress/2022/march-2022-survival-mode, (accessed June 23, 2022).

of companies are now working to shift their leadership model to a more contemplative approach. Louise Aston, wellbeing director at the business membership organization Business In The Community, says:

Wellbeing used to be positioned as a nice-to-have, fluffy bolt-on, with fruit on Fridays and lunchtime Pilates. However, wellbeing is now a strategic boardroom issue, linked to securing business objectives and driving sustainable performance and productivity. Both the business case social case are compelling, and employee wellbeing is now firmly established as a core component of responsible business. This includes the whole workforce, including the chief executive.

Companies are recognizing that the workplace is changing and that reactive leadership has left their leaders craving something more. The unprecedented stress of our times demands a new approach, and contemplative leadership is a hopeful path that promises the possibility of growth, peace, and transformation. Contemplative leaders work not just to bring immediate results, but to ensure the vitality of their employees and their organizations in an ever-changing frontier. Because the approach is rooted in the power of the inner self, contemplative leaders are motivated just as much by their own desires as by their interlocutors. Instead of developing one-sided results that prioritize winning, contemplative leaders develop results that are beneficial to *all* parties.

STRESS AND THE NEW NORMAL LEADERSHIP

Stress is recognized as the fastest-growing occupational hazard in the United States. This comes as no surprise given how fast-paced, overbooked, and demanding our modern lives were even before the pandemic changed our world. For employees at all levels of an organization, stress can contribute to:

- lack of focus
- inability to communicate
- lack of camaraderie
- physical health problems
- mental health problems
- negativity
- burnout

There are several core factors inherent in the leader's role that contribute to chronic stress and burnout, including:

- Work overload, travel, long work hours, a lack of available resources, and frequent meetings
- Distractions and time commitments not directly tied to the leader's primary responsibilities
- Relationships and interpersonal conflict with colleagues and other employees
- Work-life balance, i.e., managing the persistent demands of family and personal relationships and other life responsibilities
- Unrelenting pressure to innovate

Chronic stress and fatigue have both become so commonplace that combined, they cost the U.S. industry more than $300 billion annually in medical and insurance costs (American Psychological Association, 2020). Meanwhile, the challenges presented to organizations during the COVID-19 pandemic have shined the light on the need for organizations to address the mental health and wellbeing of their workforce more than ever.

Despite this, research conducted by the Center for Creative Leadership found that 60% of the 230 executive leaders who were surveyed admitted that their respective organizations do not provide stress management training or tools to cope with workplace stress.

ANOTHER WAY TO VIEW STRESS

Stress is a signal that occurs in times of volatility, uncertainty, chaos, and ambiguity (VUCA).[3] It is a naturally occurring *physiological* response to a change in circumstance. Like an allergic reaction, stress asks us to pay attention, to prepare, and to adapt to our environment. It should not be confused for the allergen itself which, often, we cannot control.

For several generations, we have heard that stress is a danger that must be avoided, and when it arises, it must be eradicated. This approach, however, sets us up for missed opportunities, and we fall short of our full potential. Is it possible we have been seeing stress through the wrong lens?

What would happen if we accepted stress as a natural part of our lives that came and went, flowed and stalled? What if we could answer the volatility of our emotional lives with steadfastness, uncertainty with focus, chaos with calm, and ambiguity with an open heart? What if we moved beyond the notion that *eradicating* stress is the answer and instead became skilled at shifting stress into a "state of flow?"

While the current times have tested leaders with extraordinary obstacles, they have also presented opportunities to lead with compassion, grace, and resilience. Stress may be an uncomfortable experience, but it also announces a special, sacred space. "Something significant is happening," stress tells us, "and you should pay attention. This is an important moment for you and your organization."

Contemplative leadership gives leaders the tools to explore these moments. It helps us recognize the changing circumstances and respond with a state of ease rather than resistance. In my contemplative leadership practice, I've seen that leaders who can effectively lean into stress are better able to manage people, productivity, and projects, too.

REACTIVE OR REFLECTIVE LEADERSHIP

When faced with stress or a crisis, leaders will tend to respond in one of two ways: reactively or reflectively. In my interviews with contemplative leaders, they frequently note the capacity to be more reflective. Rather than react from a place of emotion, contemplative leaders are better able to approach stressful situations with poise, calm and focus.

The literature on mindfulness and other reflective practices speaks to this idea of observing without judgment or reactivity. For the contemplative leader, moments of heightened tension and even moments of crisis appear less like raging fire and more like water: flowing.

If you are thinking this is easier said than done, you would be correct! In my own consultancy, there have been times over the years when I've felt triggered and have reacted emotionally within myself. Recently, I had an experience with an executive leader I was consulting. I felt instinctively that the client's decision would jeopardize the organization and undermine the hard work that we had done. Although I never reacted externally, I recall how upset I felt by this decision. While this is not a frequent occurrence, it does happen. We all have moments when we react—even contemplatives! What's key is having the presence of mind to catch ourselves—to recalibrate and respond more thoughtfully or reflectively.

I typically sit with myself and examine why I may have reacted the way I did. I may process the situation with a mentor or coach who can be a sounding board, provide perspective, and offer feedback. In the above situation, I realized that I had developed an attachment to the outcome of the consulting project I was working on. So, when the client made a decision that was contrary to the shared vision of the organization, I experienced an inner reaction: conflict.

We must allow ourselves to be human when we feel triggered by something or experience a momentary lapse of judgment. At the same time, it's worth noting that quick, reactive responses are vital at times—both in life and in work. Take for example what Malcolm Gladwell has to say in his famous book *Blink*:

> We tend to assume that the logical, analytical route leads to superior decisions, but whether this is accurate depends on the situation. The quick, intuitive route can be lifesaving; when we suddenly feel intense fear, a fight-or-flight response kicks in that leads to immediate action without methodically weighing all possible options and their consequences. Additionally, experienced managers can often make decisions very

quickly because experience or expertise has taught them what to do in a given situation. These managers might not be able to explain the logic behind their decision, and will instead say they just went with their "gut," or did what "felt" right. Because the manager has faced a similar situation in the past and has figured out how to deal with it, the brain shifts immediately to the quick, intuitive decision-making system.[4]

Like most things in life, leadership requires a balance between instinctive action and steady thoughtfulness, and so we must learn to strike a calm balance between the immediacy of reactive leadership and the sustenance of reflective leadership. I'll talk more about the importance of intuition and "going with your gut" in Chapter 5.

INVITATION TO PRACTICE

Preparation:

- 15 minutes of undistracted time
- A comfortable place to sit
- A journal or note book
- A pen
- A timer

Over the years, I have experimented with many breathing techniques. I have found the 4 – 7 – 8 method to be very beneficial for easing stress and feelings of overwhelm. Popularized by Harvard-trained medical doctor, Andrew Weil, it is based on an ancient yogic technique known as Pranayama. In Sanskrit, the word prana means life energy, and yama means control.

[4]Malcolm Gladwell (2005). Blink: The Power of Thinking Without Thinking. New York: Back Bay Books.

It is, therefore, a practice of breath regulation. Referred to by Dr. Weil as, "a natural tranquilizer for the nervous system," the 4 – 7 – 8 method has been shown to strengthen the connection between body and mind, promoting relaxation and present-state awareness.[5]

For this exercise, you'll want to give yourself 15 minutes. Find a comfortable place to sit that is free from distractions. Take a few moments to become relaxed and still.

LET'S BEGIN.

- Empty your lungs of air.
- Breathe in through your nose for a count of 4 seconds.
- Hold your breath for a count of 7 seconds.
- Exhale on a count of 8. When exhaling, do so audibly and with some force.
- Repeat this exercise 4 times. (If you feel comfortable, gently close your eyes.)
- Step #1 – Breathe in, for a count of 4
- Step #2 – Hold your breath for a count of 7
- Step #3 – Breathe out for a count of 8
- Repeat this 4 times.

Continuing to remain relaxed and open, take a few moments to reflect on your own experience as a leader. Think back to a time when you may have rushed to judgment or made a reactive decision about something. How did it feel to be reactive in that moment? What was the impact on you, your team, or your project? In retrospect, how could you have handled that situation differently? Please do not feel judgment or any self-criticism here.

[5] Andrew Weil, M.D., "Three Breathing Exercises and Techniques," https://www.drweil.com/health-wellness/body-mind-spirit/stress-anxiety/breathing-three-exercises/ (accessed June 23, 2022).

Set your timer to 2 minutes and write down any observations that come to you. Feel free to use your own journal or the writing space below:

Now, reflect on how you would have approached the same situation from a reflective stance. How would slowing down have helped you in your decision-making? Again, there is no judgment here. Simply invite yourself to notice the difference.

Again, set your timer to 2 minutes and write down any observations that come to you.

CONTEMPLATIVE LEADER PROFILE

Janet Drey

Managing Director, Consortium for Contemplative Leadership

The contemplative practices Janet uses in her own life include:

- daily centering prayer; silence
- Lectio Divina – sacred reading
- journaling
- Ignatian discernment and daily Examen
- walking meditation

Janet Drey is the managing director of the Consortium for Contemplative Leadership in Des Moines, Iowa—an organization that supports leaders in awakening the inner life. Since 2011, she has developed and refined a variety of programs and retreats (alone and with others) for contemplative leadership, including a nine-month leadership development program; six-week courses; ongoing small groups; MIT's U-Lab local "Hub" groups for contemplative leadership; and as a guest lecturer for an undergraduate university course on leadership.

While writing this book, I had the opportunity to sit down with Janet to learn more about her work. She described how the most important leadership tool is first and foremost the leader's self. It is therefore critical to assist leaders in becoming more conscious of who they are, as well as the motivations influencing their leadership.

Contemplation is an engagement with that self and a pathway to one's authentic voice, she explained to me. "Contemplation is primarily awareness to the present. It is the process of awakening to what various wisdom traditions have called the true or essential self, of developing habits of noticing, of experiencing ourselves as part of a larger whole, and of penetrating the illusions beneath what we identify as 'self' and 'reality.'"

Some of the benefits of contemplative leadership that Janet outlined include:

- greater emotional and spiritual intelligence
- an ever-deepening capacity to listen
- an increased ability to work with challenges and create new solutions

- an acceptance of the unknown and a trust in the eventual emergence of answers
- a reduction in reactive or "triggered" responses, even when facing uncertainty, the unexpected, and deeply ingrained patterns in one's thought and action
- openness to new ideas and a letting go of ideas that no longer serve a purpose
- greater consciousness, freedom and agility

For Janet, incorporating contemplative practice can be as easy as slipping a few small periods of silence into the busyness of the day. "At the beginning of meetings, groups can pause for a moment to let go of distractions to bring people to greater presence and openness to the collective work ahead. Pauses can be as short as a few deep breaths or several minutes. Regardless of the methods or amount of time, the benefits are often felt in less defensiveness and better decisions, as individuals and groups access their essential self and let go of ego."

Contemplative leadership is an unfolding journey of inner growth, and as Janet explains, that journey, "assists leaders in becoming more conscious of who they are and the purposes they serve, as well as of the motivations, perceptions, and worldviews that can limit or cause problems. Leaders and organizations discover a bigger purpose than serving their own desires for comfort, safety, esteem, or power. In an evolving way, contemplative leadership integrates personal and interpersonal development with organizational and social transformation."

"What we plant in the soil of contemplation, we shall reap in the harvest of action." – Meister Eckhart

CHAPTER 2

Contemplative Practices

The word "contemplate" derives from the Latin word contemplari, which means continued attention or to observe or gaze attentively. When we take that attentive gaze and turn it inwards, we are engaging in a contemplative practice. There isn't one definition for contemplative practice or a single approach; in simplest terms, it includes an array of mind-body practices such as conscious breathing, centering prayer, yoga, tai chi, qigong, and many other practices that help to quiet the mind and sustain focused attention.

All contemplative practices encourage a sense of wholeness and unity with self. They help to cultivate feelings of stillness, self-awareness, attention, empathy, improved self-regulation, and stress reduction, among other benefits. The Center for Contemplative Mind in Society describes contemplative practices as having two aims, which are foundational to all practices: "cultivating awareness and developing a stronger connection to one's inner wisdom." Contemplative practices encompass activities and rituals that are movement-based, creative, generative, relational, and ritualistic.[6]

Contemplative practices can fall into three main categories: stillness, creative-based, and movement-based. Meditation and mindfulness fall into the category of stillness and are more frequently practiced to help with calming and clearing the mind. However, there are other stillness practices, such as breathing exercises, centering prayer, affirmative prayer, silence, mantras, and visioning.

Artists or other creatives who feel drawn towards their medium understand full well the influence a creative endeavor can have on the inner self. Drawing, painting, journaling, and writing are contemplative when the practitioner is fully present with the activity.

Yoga has become the most commonly cited movement-based contemplative practice and tai chi is also well recognized in this way. Dancing, nature exploration, hiking, running, jogging, and walking are all activities that have the opportunity to be contemplative. The graphic below, which was adapted from the Tree of Contemplative Practices, created by the Center for Contemplative Mind in Society, offers an array of practices you may consider based on your preferences.

---

[6] Center for Contemplative Mind and Society, 2015.

STILLNESS	MINDFULNESS MEDITATION SILENCE CENTERING PRAYER
GENERATIVE	CONTEMPLATIVE READING LOVING-KINDNESS MEDITATION VISUALIZATION VISIONING
CREATIVE	JOURNALING DRAWING ARTISTIC EXPRESSION MUSIC NATURE
MOVEMENT	AIKIDO, TAI CHI, CHI KUNG WALKING/LABYRINTH WALKING CONTEMPLATIVE RUNNING YOGA DANCE

As you can see, there are many practices available and there are many more that are not shown here. Your daily life may already incorporate some of these practices without you realizing that you are actually engaged in a form of contemplation. For example, using your daily walk to catch up on phone calls would be multitasking and not contemplative. Leaving your phone at home and paying attention to your body and the sounds you hear for the duration of the walk, would be contemplative. Some of the practices are employed for twenty minutes or more each day while others may be practiced multiple times per day. Still, others represent a deep commitment by the practitioner to fully integrate the practice into all aspects of one's daily life and way of being.

CONSCIOUS BREATHING

Conscious breathing, or breath awareness, is foundational to contemplative practice. In Eastern traditions, the breath is a gateway to the mind. It is the simplest and most powerful way to slow down, notice, and be present. When a leader is experiencing stress or overwhelm, the breath may become shallow, and one is likely to breathe from the upper chest. Although this is a typical response to stress, it impacts the leader's ability to make sound decisions and act from a place of calm and clarity. Thus, breathing consciously is a path to effective leadership because it allows you to lead from a place of steadiness and awareness. Breathing helps you to slow down and increase your attention. In doing so, you are able to see yourself and others in a different way. Conscious breathing allows leaders to focus inward first, and then outward. It takes only moments, but it yields lasting results when practiced consistently.

It's not just the ancients who have promoted the importance of slowing the breath. Scientific studies indicate that slower breathing helps calm the nervous system and reduce cortisol levels. Individuals who incorporate simple breathing techniques into their daily regimen experience a 20%-50% increase in cognitive function.

MINDFULNESS

Mindfulness has been defined as "the awareness that emerges through paying attention on purpose, in the present moment, and non-judgmentally to the unfolding of experience moment by moment.[7]" An intention of mindfulness is to witness and observe one's emotional and physical state of being without criticism or judgment. This is often referred to as present-state awareness. In the 1st century AD, the Greek philosopher Epictetus noticed how the mind distorted our ability to perceive. "People are disturbed not by a thing," he wrote, "but by their perception of a thing." The intention of mindfulness is to witness and observe one's emotional and physical state of being without judgment or framing.

The introduction of mindfulness was fostered by the popularization of Zen Buddhism in the United States in the 1950s and 1960s. In the early 1970s, mindfulness was promulgated by the revered Buddhist Monk, Thich Nhat Hanh, who garnered the respect and admiration of many Western practitioners. By 1979, mindfulness was introduced by Dr. Jon Kabat-Zinn as a therapeutic intervention for stress. Although mindfulness derives from Buddhist teachings, it should be noted that it stands alone as a therapeutic modality, untethered by religious underpinnings.

---

[7] Jon Kabat-Zinn (2003). Mindfulness-based interventions in context: past, present, and future. Clin. Psychol. Sci. Pract. 10, 144–156

The late Francisco Varela, a respected neuroscientist and meditation practitioner, believed that human beings act from a place of patterned, habitual responses rather than from a place of conscious awareness. He believed that human beings have a tendency to be reflexive and act without consideration of our actions, regardless of the effects those actions may incur. Varela hypothesized that mindful awareness creates a space to allow individuals to choose more deliberately and consciously, thus regulating emotion and behavior.

Harvard Business School professor and former CEO of Medtronic, Bill George, stresses the unique value of mindfulness for professional leaders. "Mindfulness enables leaders to be fully present, aware of themselves and their impact on other people, and sensitive to their reactions to stressful situations," he writes. "Leaders who are mindful tend to be more effective in understanding and relating to others, and in motivating them toward shared goals." Indeed, mindfulness practices are known to relieve stress, enhance focus, boost creativity, improve productivity, and increase emotional intelligence for improved work relationships.

It's not surprising that a recent article in the Harvard Business Review pointed out that mindfulness is on the rise in America's workplaces. A growing number of leaders and organizations are discovering the benefits of contemplative practices and offering opportunities for employees to engage in mindfulness, meditation, yoga, and other contemplative practices. There is a growing constellation of contemplatively-oriented companies are incorporating mindfulness into their offices, including General Mills, Proctor and Gamble, Target, and Sony. Marc Benioff, founder and CEO of Salesforce has invested heavily in promoting and providing space for mindfulness practices for his employees. The company's offices are equipped with meditation rooms, and team members are actively encouraged to take daily time from their duties to unplug and meditate. Other employers, such as Green Mountain Coffee, offer incentives to employees who take time during their workday to perform activities that add to their happiness. The company's CEO, Bob Stiller, believes this is a key driver of job performance.

Additionally, many high-profile executives credit mindfulness and meditation with their ability to lead and achieve high results, and they speak willingly and publicly on the subject. Some of these include Bill Gates, Oprah Winfrey, Ariana Huffington, and Jerry Seinfeld, to name a few. Mindfulness is an integral component to the broader contemplative practices utilized by a growing number of leaders.

THE SCIENCE OF MINDFULNESS

I would be remiss if I did not include the biological benefits of contemplative practice as it relates to the brain. Neuroplasticity is a term that describes the brain's ability to change in response to experiences throughout the lifespan. There are different processes that stimulate the growth of new neural connections and brain cells. Scientific inquiry on the neurophysiological benefits of contemplative practice has been evolving over the past decade. Mindfulness, meditation, and other mental training practices help to promote changes in the brain that contribute to psychological health and well-being.

While each person will have a uniquely subjective experience with mindfulness or meditation, chances are you will feel more peaceful, balanced, less reactive, and less emotional. You will feel more integrated and whole. Dr. Dan Siegel, psychiatry professor at the UCLA School of Medicine and director of the Mindful Awareness Research Center, writes that contemplative practices such as mindfulness "develop a higher degree of integration" in the brain.[8] A brain that is well-integrated possesses strong neural connections in the prefrontal region, which experts say is the seat of conscious awareness. A well-integrated brain has a greater capacity for adaptability and is more receptive to change. Through repeated daily practice, the brain grows new neurons, it strengthens synaptic connections, and it promotes faster connections. The practice of mindfulness, and meditation in particular, helps re-wire the brain so it can regulate emotions and cool its reactivity to perceived threats.

This may explain why the majority of the participants in my doctoral study responded to stress and organizational uncertainty with such remarkable ease. It would appear that their shared experiences are natural occurrences based on the neurological changes taking place in specific regions of the brain. As referenced previously, mindful awareness creates a space that allows individuals to choose more deliberately and consciously. Once again, Viktor Frankl's quote is fitting here: "Between stimulus and response, there is a space. In that space is our power to choose our response. In our response lies our growth and our freedom." By bringing one's attention to the range of choices that are available to us, we can experience impulses without engaging them. With practice, we learn to respond differently to impulsivity. The more space we create, the greater our awareness and ability to choose in the moment.

---

[8] Dr. Dan Siegel, "On Integration as a Source of Strength." https://www.youtube.com/watch?v=0TK62FdzzTs (accessed June 23, 2022).

Recent research reveals that eight weeks of mindfulness meditation for ten to fifteen minutes a day can produce these results
and lower the amygdala's response to emotional stimuli. This
research is heartening and shows how simple it is to make significant changes to our lives with just a small "dose" of contemplative practice. For lasting impact, however, leaders should consider contemplation as a continuous, unbounded way of life—a
lifelong path to self-realization.

INVITATION TO PRACTICE CONTEMPLATION

For this exercise, you'll just need 10 to 15 minutes. You can take
notes in the pages here or in your own journal. Grab a pen, and
find a comfortable place to sit that is free from distractions. Take
a few moments to become relaxed and still. We'll continue using
the 4-7-8 breathing pattern to help you quiet your mind and
move into a state of deeper relaxation.

LET'S BEGIN.

- Empty your lungs of air
- Breathe in through your nose for a count of 4 seconds
- Hold your breath for a count of 7 seconds
- Exhale on a count of 8. When exhaling, do so audibly
  and with some force
- Repeat this exercise 4 times (if you feel comfortable,
  gently close your eyes)

In this state of relaxation and openness, please jot down any
contemplative activities, rituals, or practices that you engage in
regularly and explore how those practices benefit you and your
ability to be present as a leader.

If you do not currently have a contemplative practice, did any of the practices pique your interest? If so, consider taking some time to learn more about that particular practice to see how you like it. You may try and decide, for whatever reason, that it's not for you. It's not uncommon for people to have a formal meditation practice and include other practices as part of daily rituals. You'll see in the contemplative leaders' profiles that each person has multiple practices that support their quality of being.

Please take a few moments to write down practices you want to try. This may take a little time, so be patient with yourself through this journey.

_____

_____

_____

_____

_____

_____

_____

_____

_____

_____

_____

_____

_____

_____

_____

_____

"With mindfulness, you can establish yourself in the present in order to touch the wonders of life that are available in that moment" – Thich Nhat Hanh

CHAPTER 3

Qualities of Contemplative Leadership

To fully appreciate the mutual relationship between contemplation and leadership, it is important to understand just how central the leader's self is to his or her quality of leadership. In my 20 years of coaching leaders, I have come to understand that a leader's inner-self is the most important leadership tool. How a leader perceives, behaves, interacts, communicates, and ultimately leads is shaped by the leader's inner being and their relationship to that being.

Recent leadership studies have taken an interest in the inner life of the leader by examining key qualities that build resilience and effective leadership, especially during times of change and uncertainty. My own research supports these findings, revealing how contemplation helps cultivate essential leadership skills.

Below I share some of these skills. The list is not meant to be exhaustive. Rather, it represents the more salient qualities derived from contemplative practice.

SELF AWARENESS

In my interviews with contemplative leaders, self-awareness was considered the foundation for effective leadership and a prerequisite for the other qualities discussed below. A growing body of leadership studies recognizes the importance of self-awareness as an essential quality that helps leaders think critically, solve problems, identify blind spots, and regulate emotions. For example, leaders who have a high degree of self-awareness are more in tune with their own reactions to others and their interactions in the organization. MIT systems scientist and founder of the Society for Organizational Learning, Peter Senge, believes that self-reflection is essential to leadership. "Leaders should be people who are deeply involved in their own realization of being a human being," he states and goes on to speak of leaders being clear about their own inner psychology.

Having a greater sense of self-awareness is an essential component of emotional intelligence and effective leadership. It allows leaders to gain access to alternative ways of seeing their world. Maria Gonzalez, author of *Mindful Leadership*, shares that self-awareness allows leaders to "maintain sound judgment and make better decisions because moment by moment you'll see what is arising within you."[9] Self-aware leaders:

- Have a clear, realistic understanding of their capabilities, strengths, and weaknesses that is in keeping with the opinion of those they lead

---

[9] Maria Gonzalez (2012). Mindful Leadership: 9 Ways to Self-Awareness, Transforming Yourself, and Inspiring Others. Jossey-Bass.

- Accept that their idea is one of many and welcome diverse opinions and thoughts from team members
- Routinely solicit feedback from others at every level of the organization Take responsibility for their own mishaps
- Are better able to act consistently with their values and principles
- Display behavior that is congruent and aligned with core values
- Have an increased sense of attentiveness

EMPATHY

One may not initially associate empathy with leadership, particularly in competitive and fast-paced work environments. Empathy is often left overlooked as a leadership quality, but in times of challenge or crisis, it is an attribute of significant importance.

Empathy is simply defined as the ability to understand and share the feelings of others. It differs from sympathy in a seemingly small, but significant, way. With sympathy, we express concern and care for another, but we don't attempt to really see and understand their plight from their perspective. Empathy calls on us to put ourselves in another person's shoes and imagine what they must be feeling and contending with due to a particular circumstance or event. While sympathy can be synonymous with pity, empathy goes much deeper. Empathy asks a person to relate to another person's emotional experience entirely, with awareness and understanding of the full spectrum of human emotions.

The pandemic was a summons to look at one another as humans, with whole, complex lives, in a way we never had before, and to bear witness to the reality that we are all connected. It required that we develop empathy for each other and adjust to a new working model that could create synergy between people's home lives and their work lives. The line between the two is getting fuzzier all the time, and working from home has never been more common. Organizations have embraced this new way of doing business as they have discovered that a more flexible work-home model boosts both productivity and morale.

Gone is the American work culture that demanded an employee leave their personal lives at the door. Instead, today's professional leaders need to understand how to access empathy for their colleagues' personal lives and how to sustain it. Today's human workers are, above all, human beings who can no sooner fully separate their work and personal lives than the sun could separate heat from light.

Empathy, a trait exhibited by those with higher emotional intelligence, is a powerful quality that allows leaders to:

- Have lower turnover on their teams
- Receive positive evaluations from their staff
- Demonstrate active listening in interactions with staff
- Allow team members the autonomy needed to complete tasks and projects
- Look for ways to advance the skillset, achievement, and productivity of team members
- Create inclusive, problem-solving solutions for projects that are struggling
- Exude warmth and approachability
- Encourage team members to problem-solve independently and avoid micro-managing.

- Actively listen and respond to team member concerns or challenges.

Empathy is often discussed as a predetermined personality trait as if we are either born empathetic or not. There is certainly some truth to this in the same way that some people are naturally introverted and others are outgoing extroverts, but empathy *can* be practiced, cultivated, and honed. There is a growing interest in the notion of empathy as an essential leadership quality, but until recently, very few organizations or schools focused on teaching empathy or incorporating empathy training. Contemplative practices help open the heart and the mind towards an empathic approach to the world.

PRESENT-STATE AWARENESS

The practice of "living in the moment" is found in many cultures throughout human history, and being present is another fundamental quality at the heart of contemplative practice. The quality of being present allows leaders to be more in the moment and thus available to themselves and their employees. We have all had experiences during which we were physically *present* but our minds were somewhere else. We may nod and mutter words of acknowledgement from time to time to indicate that we are listening but if the person we are supposedly engaged with asked us to answer a specific question or provide an opinion, we would have nothing to say because we aren't *actually* listening. In fact, we aren't actually there at all. We are elsewhere in our minds, lost in worry, mulling future plans, ruminating about the past, or simply wandering. Being fully present is about being actively engaged only in what is happening right now. This is easier said than done.

We all have circumstances that can temporarily drive us to distraction. Life happens, and even leaders must acknowledge their own humanness. However, if a leader does not intentionally adopt a state of present-state awareness, their ability to inspire, and connect with others can be hindered. Contemplative leaders actively look for ways to tune into this state because they understand the importance of being fully present in all of their interactions.

Further, a leader who can cultivate present-state awareness will be more easily able to enter a state of flow, which is a quality I discuss in a few pages. The extent to which a leader is present or not impacts their own performance and work experience and that of those they lead in myriad ways. Leaders who immerse themselves in present-state awareness are better able to:

- Actively listen and respond to the needs and concerns of their team
- Be in control of their own thoughts
- Have the ability to analyze detailed information in real time
- Encourage input and ideas from people at all levels of the organization
- Receive positive feedback from team members related to their ability to connect with team members in meaningful ways
- Adopt new routines and processes to move fluidly with change
- Leave people with the impression that they have been heard and understood after engaging with them
- Resist checking email or their phone during meetings or conversations with others

- Reflect meaningfully on their own performance or behaviors

Whether you have fallen prey to the ceaseless opportunities for distraction yourself or have been involved in conversations with others in which you knew the person was not really participating with you, it's easy to relate to the problems that can come along as a result of not being fully present. On the flip side, we all know what it feels like to leave an interaction, even if it was a difficult situation, feeling heard. Present-moment awareness is a gift that can be delivered from leaders to team members with kindness and sincerity.

LEADERSHIP AGILITY

One of the hardest things we face in our lives is accepting that two things can be true at the same time. We are wired to believe that duality represents a contradiction. And yet, life proves again and again that we must find room in ourselves to accept not just one end of a duality, but both. In a work environment, for example, we need to accept that we are individuals and team members at one and the same time. We must be confident and humble, ambitious and relaxed, limited and unlimited, inclusive and circumscribed, professional and human. The challenges of this tug-of-war may resonate especially with people of color and women who feel, every day, the professional demand to seamlessly present multiple identities in all aspects of their work lives.

As we try to understand how to interpret the divergent poles of our experiences and how to behave accordingly, we wonder constantly if our actions have gone too far in one direction or if we've alienated some people to please others. This can create feelings of enormous anxiety, and as this anxiety builds, it can have devastating effects. Some of course include panic attacks, depression, insomnia, verbal and physical outbursts, substance use, relational difficulties, and more.

Contemplative practices give leaders the chance to step away from this whirlwind of confusion and to breathe—literally and figuratively. By taking a chance to sit with the truest, deepest self, contemplative leaders are given the gift of agility. They can deftly move through ambiguity with ease and grace, and they can better understand that contradictions are not meant to be moments of discord, but rather moments of harmony. Through pause and reflection, the notes of the symphony come together; instead of making noise, they make, at last, a kind of music. Sounds are now fresh and illuminating and help a leader understand their path clearly. In the place of confusion, a leader now sees opportunities for innovation and unity.

Agile leaders experience:

- Increased ability to resolve conflicts so that all parties feel valued
- Improved empathy towards others
- Reduced anxiety and its attendant symptoms
- Reduced shame and self-recrimination
- Improved energy management

LETTING GO OF EGO

The leaders I've interviewed have mentioned how their respective practices help them to be more authentic and to lead from a non-egoic place. A key leadership challenge of our age is to transform *ego-system awareness into ecosystem awareness*. This process is about transcending individualistic working environments that prize the ideas, strategy, and execution of the individual leader, and embracing egoless systems that foster collaborative leadership and community among team members.

Contemplative leadership asks leaders to cultivate an awareness of ego and to become personally dedicated to leading from a more expanded place. Being aware of our ego and the impact it can have on us as leaders is a building block to authentic leadership. Leaders who transcend ego are better able to look beyond their individual needs to see the bigger picture. They understand that they are a part of something greater than themselves and are keenly aware of how their actions impact others. Contemplative leaders are not driven by power. Instead, they empower others and distribute power for the greater good of their organization.

Leading from an expanded level of consciousness, contemplatives take in a great deal of information, synthesize it, remove their personal bias from it, and make decisions based upon it that are best for the organization, not just for themselves. Rising above individualism and egocentrism in the service of the organization (or collective) requires humility and a continuous process of self-evaluation. Having the courage to reveal one's truth, and to be vulnerable, is neither an easy nor linear process. You'll have moments when you feel connected and self-aware, and you'll also have moments when you feel separated or disconnected and find yourself sliding into ego-consciousness. In those moments, I urge you to pause and notice. This is the ebb and flow of life itself. By devoting oneself to a reflective practice inward, the ego will gradually dissolve and loosen its grip. This process gives sway to a larger, truer Self—a gradual, transformative process that brings forward an authentic way of leading.

Contemplative leaders who have a healthy relationship with their ego are better able to:

- Make decisions that are for the best of the organization, not themselves
- Solicit feedback from peers and team members and use it to become better
- Actively seek input and ideas from others as well as delegate responsibilities
- Be vulnerable and show their authentic selves to those they serve
- Receive their team members' ideas, work, and abilities with a sincere openness
- Stay humble and able to admit their own mistakes
- Willingly perform all duties without seeing any as "beneath" them
- Engage in discussions with an open, authentic curiosity
- Value being in right relationship with others

HEART AND MIND COHERENCE

When the thoughts in our minds align with the feelings in our heart, something very powerful occurs. In fact, it is the most powerful thing of all. Heart and mind coherence is what happens when we think, speak, and act our highest truth, sacrificing nothing and being fully authentic. A leader exemplifies this unity when they lead with their true self.

You may be surprised to learn that the heart and mind connection is not just an emotional one. Our hearts actually contain neural tissue that communicates directly with the brain. The commonly held belief that the brain inside our skulls is the master system sending instructions to the rest of the body is not exactly right. The HeartMath Institute, a non-profit in California, is dedicated to helping leaders better understand the heart-brain connection. Their research reveals that there is a very complex system of nerves within the heart that sends signals to the brain with more frequency than it receives signals from the brain. The heart and mind are not just spiritually connected—they are physiologically connected, too.

The leader who can align their heart with their mind will be honest with others and, most importantly, with themselves. This fearless embrace of the truth has profound implications. Authenticity ranks high on the list of desirable traits between a leader and their followers, and for good reason. Saying one thing and doing another breeds confusion and distrust. Further, when the contemplative leader takes actions that are in sync with their heart and their mind, they need not worry. They need not dwell or ruminate because they have clarity on what they are doing.

Overall, heart and mind coherence supports the leader's resilience. We understand that the ability to carry on and continue leading, even under tenuous and trying circumstances, is an imperative in the modern workplace. Removing the conflict between heart and mind and finding your true self teaches your brain that no matter what, you are going to be okay.

When the going gets tough, which it inevitably will, the contemplative leader draws on their practice to find their footing, regain balance, and act from a place of grounded composure.

Heart and mind coherence allows leaders to:

- Synergize and collaborate more effectively with others
- Reduce conflict within themselves and with team members
- Break through negative or outmoded thinking patterns
- Let go of the past to make future-proof business decisions

FLOW

"Flow state" was coined by Hungarian-American psychologist Mihaly Csikszentmihalyi. It is a state in which you are "completely involved in an activity for its own sake." This feeling is often described as being "in the zone." It involves a sense of fluidity between body and mind where time seems to slow down and you are totally absorbed beyond the possibility of distraction. Present-state awareness is a requisite for reaching a state of flow. The flow state is thought to be the optimal state to achieve heightened productivity and creativity. Flow states make the work feel easy and delightful, boosting performance and adding greatly to a person's sense of fulfillment and happiness in their work.

Research shows that flow states are associated with human biology and, specifically, with brain chemistry. When we are in a flow state, there is a release of performance-enhancing chemicals including dopamine, norepinephrine, serotonin, and endorphins. These "feel-good" chemicals fuel intrinsic motivation and help us to focus, making the processing of information easier and promoting intuition beyond normal-conscious awareness. This same altering of the chemistry in the brain also activates the relaxation response. Brain waves are slowed to effectively reduce stress and anxiety. This phenomenon is linked to increased creativity and focus as it creates space to decompress and release tension.

Chances are you have experienced a flow state and can relate to just how easy and natural it can feel in the moment. But it doesn't have to be left up to chance. If we can intentionally make space for the release of tension, stress, and anxiety, we can open the doors to a state of flow whenever we need, thus opening the possibility of an optimal state of focus and performance. Internal space is created through practices that any leader can incorporate into their life. For both individuals and organizations alike, the quality of work experience can be transformed with the incorporation of flow in daily work life. For leaders, a flow state can give you a significant competitive advantage, with benefits including:

For leaders, flow state can give you a significant competitive advantage, with benefits including:

- Higher productivity
- Lower turnover rate
- Greater business profit
- Increased mental clarity
- Creativity and new sparks of imagination
- Accelerated learning and skill development
- Increased customer and employee satisfaction

ENERGY MANAGEMENT

As humans, we are little ecosystems, shaped by the ebb and flow of our seasons. We have our very own winters when we must retreat and restore; we have our summers when we grow and we create. We plant, we harvest, we spend, we store. A leader with a contemplative center is able to read these seasons and respond appropriately. They are able to understand their emotional weathervanes and watch out for storms.

It is through self-awareness that contemplative leaders are able to know when their energy level will be high, low, or in-between. Further, they are aware of what triggers, events, or circumstances impact their energy level. They use this information and awareness to plan their schedule for optimal performance. Meetings, tasks, and routines are intentionally planned around expected energy levels. Travel schedules, strategy sessions, and solitary tasks are all viewed through the lens of the leader's energy reserves and are scheduled accordingly. If an unexpected circumstance impacts the contemplative leader's energy level or reserve, the contemplative leader will make tweaks to the schedule to maximize results. As energy management relates to planning, the focus lies squarely on the leader's management of *energy*, not on the management of their *time*. It's a subtle, but significant distinction.

Accessing one's energy to channel it into the challenge at hand is another component to effective energy management. Despite our best efforts, there will be unanticipated distractions, conditions, and circumstances that impact the leader's ability to access their energy when it is needed most. Through contemplative practices, we can become better equipped to regain our composure when something knocks us off-center. We can bring our minds and bodies into a balanced state, in relatively short order, opening the channel to our energy reserves and applying it to the work at hand. The contemplative leader has a variety of methods available to them. Some of the methods discussed in this book include meditation, or breathing techniques, which can be employed wherever and whenever they are needed.

The final component to energy management is restoration. Energy restoration happens daily with nourishing food choices, sound sleep schedules, attention to personal relationships, and of course, contemplative practices. There is also clear justification for taking regular time away from the role as a leader to spend more significant chunks of time refilling your energy wells. Long weekends, vacations, and even sabbaticals can pay energy dividends that far exceed the time allotted to taking them.

Leadership is improved by effective energy management in many ways, including:

- Increased productivity
- Reduced stress, overwhelm, and burn out for the leader and the team
- Improved well being physically, emotionally, and mentally
- Reduced turnover and improved job satisfaction
- Empowering individuals to organize and produce work in line with their personal rhythms, fostering a culture focused on wellness for all

OPEN MINDEDNESS

An open-mind is more receptive to the ideas put forth by others, even when those ideas do not immediately synchronize with that of the leader. Open mindedness ignites a curiosity within the mind of the contemplative leader, searching for understanding, common ground, and new areas fertile for exploration.

Open-minded leaders tend to be more flexible and creative, leading to improved abilities to innovate as well as to gain trust from the team members they serve. They recognize that they will have some of the answers, but not all of them. They are open to suggestions, corrections, and learning opportunities to make sound, fact-based decisions. The open mind can be changed, while the closed mind is fixed and unwilling to move. Contemplative leaders who regularly turn inward are better able to open themselves up to the rest of the world, embrace change, and make progress.

Open-minded leaders more frequently:

- Experience lower turnover rates among team members
- Discover innovative solutions to prickly problems
- Act intentionally with honest observation of emotions
- Receive positive feedback from team members who feel supported and heard

These qualities grow from the heart of the leader outward, cultivating a contemplative garden of respect and organic engagement among team members. This creates powerful change within the culture of the organization, emanating even to the larger industry. In the next chapter, I'll discuss how our personal journeys of contemplative practice create lasting, widening ripples across the human family.

AN INVITATION TO PRACTICE

For this exercise, you'll just need 10 to 15 minutes. You can use the pages here to take notes or you can use your own journal. Grab a pen, and find a comfortable place to sit that is free from distractions. Take a few moments to become relaxed and still.

We'll continue using the 4 – 7 – 8 breathing pattern to help you quiet your mind and move into a state of deeper relaxation.

LET'S BEGIN.

- Empty your lungs of air.
- Breathe in through your nose for a count of 4 seconds.
- Hold your breath for a count of 7 seconds.
- Exhale on a count of 8. When exhaling, do so audibly and with some force.
- Repeat this exercise 4 times (if you feel comfortable, gently close your eyes).

In this state of relaxation and openness, please reflect on 2 or 3 of the qualities listed in this chapter that result from reflective practice.

As you were reading, which of the qualities resonated most with you?

If you were to cultivate that particular quality, how would that impact you, your leadership effectiveness, and your interpersonal relationships with team members?

Please take a few moments to jot down some reflections.

If there are qualities not listed here that you would like to develop, please write them down as well. Consider which contemplative practice will support you in cultivating that particular quality.

CONTEMPLATIVE LEADER PROFILE

Kim Nolan PhD

Program Chair, Mindful Leadership, Atlantic University
Buddhist Chaplain and Lifelong Activist for Social Justice

The contemplative practices Kim uses in her own life include:

- shamatha / shiné - calm abiding meditation
- nature reflection
- bearing witness practice
- community-based service and chaplaincy
- various Vajrayana practices

For over 30 years, **Kim Nolan** has worked closely with community members, leaders, and diverse teams to create engaged spaces, workplaces, and learning environments that make a positive impact on the world. She is an ordained Buddhist chaplain and a lifelong advocate for human rights. She is also the founder and executive director of the Dignity Foundation, through which she teaches self-care and mindfulness in schools and human service agencies and provides coaching to leaders seeking contemplative practice. A community-based leader, educator, and practitioner, she facilitates collaborative processes across teams, building safe relationships and achieving desired outcomes within larger systems.

I have long admired Kim's work and her beautiful, reflective writing. As I set out to develop this book, I knew I wanted to interview her to share some of her insights. "Contemplative practice is a disciplined act that bridges the sacred and mundane," she told me. "It can be embodied in everyday life. Chaplaincy work, teaching, writing, walking the dog, or drinking a hot cup of coffee can be a contemplative practice just as naturally as holding space with someone who is dying or bearing witness to grief and loss. It is not the nature of the act or experience itself, but the state of mind that makes it contemplative." She went on to say that contemplative practices are "whatever makes [a person] feel the most whole" in any circumstance, event, or task.

Regarding leadership specifically, she spoke of how a contemplative leader values the inherent wholeness of others. "This viewpoint allows the cultivation of a work or learning environment where individuals can thrive and performance can prosper," she said. "Team members who view their work as a vocation to which they were called are more likely to approach their work with reverence than employees who view their work mainly as a means to satisfy financial obligations. Students who feel seen, heard, and loved–no matter who they are and what truth they hold to be self-evident–are more likely to approach their learning with an open mind, tuned into impacts beyond their own lives and experiences." Society makes us believe there is a separateness between our human selves and the spiritual realm. But this divide can be bridged. "Those who can practice turning inward in a courageous and fearless way are taking the active steps that are absolutely necessary to reclaiming our own potential," Kim told me. She believes this integration that occurs when we dissolve this illusion of separateness is missing from leadership modeling and preparation and that a fundamental shift in our societal and cultural perspective on leadership is needed.

She proposes that leadership training be expanded to include the cultivation of traits that express contemplative leadership. "Instead of pointing to external circumstances and outcomes as being the optimal path to leadership development, the focus should turn to the internal view of the developing leader." A significant obstacle to the progress of leadership development from within, however, is the divisive nature of the word spirituality itself. In our society, the term is often thought of as synonymous with religion, though the two are not the same in Kim's view. While religion is concerned with faith and doctrine, spirituality involves how one connects to oneself and to the surrounding world. Kim asserts that spirituality is "intended to be a process of illumination, bringing light to the whole of one's development." As we slowly progress towards a wider adoption of this view, spirituality finds relevance in the workplace where it once would have been viewed as inappropriate.

Kim has conducted rich and exhaustive research aimed at addressing the question, "What is called into being for the contemplative leader?" Findings of her research suggest there are eight key qualities that are embodied in the contemplative leader.

These eight C's represent an integrative model of contemplative leadership on a whole:

1. Calling
2. Compassion
3. Care for Others
4. Centered Communication
5. Cultivate Stillness
6. Clarity
7. Currency of Time (Now)
8. Contagious Joy

This model can serve as a framework in the modeling and teaching of leadership in this new paradigm. It can find the inward path forward and lead to greater outcomes that can be measured externally in an organization setting.

"Mindful leadership aims to develop self-aware and
compassionate leaders." – Bill George

CHAPTER 4

Towards a Contemplative Work Culture

Contemplative practices are not only transformative for the individual practitioner. When operationalized, a contemplative leader's practice can help shape a more mindful culture as a whole. As a leader brings contemplative practices into their own life, their behavior sends ripple effects throughout their organization. Everything from meetings to hiring practices can begin to change. One of the most noticeable transformations is in how contemplative leaders approach power. Understanding now the interconnectivity of all parts, they seek to empower and uplift the people around them, fostering a sense of community and camaraderie. They see their organization as a collective partnership for a common cause, and they eagerly encourage leadership in all.

QUALITIES OF CONTEMPLATIVE TEAMS

What type of organizational culture do you and your team wish to create? Given the increased demands that have been placed on teams, my hunch is that team members may be yearning for a mental and emotional spaciousness that allows them to connect more deeply to themselves. They long for silence in a noisy world and respite from the busyness of their daily lives. In my interviews with senior leaders and directors who have a contemplative practice, they shared with me some of the benefits their personal practices have had on their organization as a whole. I've heard inspiring stories of leaders who took steps to transform their work culture—a process that does not happen overnight. One example is CEO Marvin Riley of industrial technology company EnPro Industries. He and his leadership team implemented organization-wide practices that promoted well-being and self-awareness among their employees. The company incorporated practices into its work culture such as meditation, mindfulness, journaling, and active listening. Team meetings began opening with moments of silence, a centering exercise, or expressions of gratitude. At the time of my meeting with Marvin, EnPro's revenues were close to two billion dollars, and they had received the Safest Company in America award three times. He credits this success to his team's individual practices and processes.

This is just one example of how contemplatively-oriented leadership has the potential to transform work culture, improve interpersonal relationships, and enhance employee wellness—all while adding to the bottom line. However, it is not necessary for leaders to restructure their entire workplaces; instead, I invite leaders to start by taking small steps.

I encourage leaders to be intentional with introducing contemplative practices into their workplaces, as they see fit. This may include offering yoga classes, including mindfulness as a part of a wellness initiative, or creating space in the office for a quiet room. Invite team members into this process and openly share the type of organizational culture you envision. You might be surprised to discover that some of your teammates have been using reflective practices in their own lives for years!

Below I share some of the ways a contemplative practice can benefit teams, whether because of a contemplative leader at the helm, or because of organizational practices as a whole.

TEAM COHESION AND COLLABORATION

In a contemplative-oriented work culture, the team understands they are serving something larger than themselves. Their actions are intimately intertwined, and they understand they are working together towards a shared vision. To reach their common goals, they must respect each others' points of view and work through differences in meaningful, sustainable ways. Everyone is equally vital to the whole organization and is a leader in their own right.

In this professional culture, the self is experienced as a multi-faceted reflection of everyone in the organization. Individual success and failure are little more than mirages. Contemplative teams understand that the professional outcomes of their collaboration are shared at every level.

This improved cohesion reduces the unhappy act of finger-pointing. When things go wrong, as at times they inevitably do, people are less likely to blame each other or to single out a scapegoat.

Instead, they pool their energy towards understanding how they can fix the problem and improve. Free of the burden of blame and the paranoia of being called next, their creative minds can open, risk-free, towards innovative solutions. Powerful things happen when people are allowed to problem-solve without recrimination.

Similarly, when things go right for an organization, the entire team is able to experience the joy together. No team member needs to feel excluded from the celebration; nor does any team member need to suppress their joy for the sake of others. This shared happiness is a powerful morale-booster, and individuals who might otherwise feel a pang of bitterness at the success of colleagues find themselves heading home at night with a sense of fulfillment. Life takes on meaning when we feel we've contributed to something larger than ourselves, and cohesive teams allow people to thrive and to look forward to thriving some more.

COMFORT WITH AMBIGUITY

As I discussed in the previous chapter, ambiguity is one of the hardest feelings to navigate. It is also one of the most common. Contemplative leaders imbue teams with continual reminders that ambiguity is not something to give us panic. Instead, it is an opportunity for us to be still and to listen.

Adjusting to ambiguity becomes especially important during moments of conflict. When we disagree, we think our own position is perfectly stark. We are certain it couldn't be more clear! But we look in front of us, and all we see is fog. The person or people talking at us are incoherent and plain absurd, we think. Contemplative leadership urges us to sit with this feeling until we begin to see clarity. We learn to listen more than to talk, to ask questions more than to answer. In doing so, the fog slowly (sometimes quickly!) begins to clear, and we start to understand what our interlocutor is trying to tell us.

This is a great step forward. Contemplative practices allow us to go deeper still. With patience, we are often able to see a strange world in which both of us are right. How can this be and what does one do?

It's easy to imagine this kind of conflict in a setting when we are engaging with others. This same tension, however, often rears itself inside of our own inner thoughts. How can we feel two things at once, and what are we supposed to do about it?

One of the most fruitful tools that contemplative leadership brings to a team is the skill of recognizing ambiguity and resisting the need to divide it into factions: right v. wrong, us v. them, profitable v. unprofitable, and so on. When teams know that it's okay to live with ambiguity and that it's possible even to thrive within it, their creative faculties open in new ways. They approach problems from innovative new angles, they treat their colleagues with fresh openness, they forgive themselves, and they forgive others.

From this new space, they are able to work together on creating the concrete solutions that polarized factions could not see in their agitated states.

MINDFUL SPACES

Today, many organizations have a designated space where employees can meditate or sit quietly at an optional time. Some companies with these areas include Google, Apple, Nike, and Salesforce, to name a few, and the spaces are an excellent way of encouraging contemplative practice among team members. The spaces can be used for group yoga, guided meditations, and other team activities as desired, and they serve as physical reminders of a company's contemplative belief system.

Indeed, the physical design of offices plays a valuable role in team-building. Office design should be intentional, keeping in mind the responsibilities of each person who will occupy a particular space. Fresh air, natural light, living plants, noise-reduction panels, and inviting colors can all contribute to how a team functions within its physical working environment.

When team members see their organization making these kinds of thoughtful adjustments to the workspace, they feel valued.

Research on office design is ever-changing, with some companies embracing open-floor plans and others favoring more compartmentalized environments. Leaders should be mindful of their team's best work habits, and if they choose an open-floor plan, they should be sure to create private spaces for people to work in silence, as needed.

MINDFUL MEETINGS

Anyone who knows me professionally is aware that I do not like having my time wasted. As a result, I try very hard not to waste people's time inviting them to meetings that I am unprepared for—this is perhaps one of my greatest pet peeves. In my work, I frequently hear people bemoan the pointlessness of meetings. When meetings are haphazardly thrown together and do not have an intention or focus they result in a lack of productivity.

A carefully, consciously planned meeting is a gift of kindness to one's team. By bringing mindfulness into our professional meetings, we bring presence, focus, and attention to our gatherings and show our teammates that we value their most important asset: their time. As a result, attendees will contribute their attention thoughtfully, and the organization will reap the rewards of improved results. At least 24 hours before the meeting begins, the meeting facilitator should distribute the intention of the meeting and its specific agenda so attendees are able to plan accordingly.

An effective way to get all meeting participants focused at the beginning of a meeting is to engage the group in a short meditation. Some corporate leaders call this kind of guided meditation a "minute to arrive" while others simply call it a "silent moment." Whatever the name, the idea is the same. The meeting facilitator should spend a full minute guiding participants to become quiet, centered, and present.

Another way to allow participants to become focused and to enjoy a more impactful meeting is to ask each attendee to share something for which they are grateful. This can be around the topic of the meeting or can be totally open-ended. Some teams use a "gratitude rock" or similar item and pass it from person to person as thoughts are shared. Alternatively, meeting attendees could simply share something that is going on in their personal lives to build connection and compassion within the group. There are creative ways this can be done virtually as well.

In my work, I enjoy starting meetings with an intention and an invitation to stillness. I am currently consulting with a Muslim organization that opens and closes each meeting with prayer, and I've previously consulted with a Quaker team that opens their meetings with silence. Your own organization may have something very unique that can help center its team before starting a meeting.

After this calm opening, the meeting leader should share a set of explicit expectations for meeting etiquette and participation. Again, this is an act of kindness as some people may not know the correct etiquette and would hate to find out they offended. Some etiquette I recommend is for phones, food, and other sources of distraction to be left out of the space, whether in person or virtually. If laptops are necessary, ask everyone to only open programs or documents relevant to the discussion at hand. Make it clear that every person who was invited to attend the meeting has something valuable to contribute and that all voices will be heard. Clearly vocalize the intention of the meeting and ask participants if they need any clarity on why the meeting is being held. This intention should have been shared previously when the agenda was distributed, but it should be expressed again with the gathered group.

Finally, make sure participants know if they should share their comments freely throughout the meeting, or if they should wait until an appropriate invitation. Different meetings will likely have different norms, and commenting at the "wrong" time can create chaos and tension in the group. It can also cause a meeting to get bloated and side-tracked, and participants will likely feel their time is being squandered.

It's worth noting that hosting a meeting is a skill and one that should be practiced and re-worked with patience and intention. Some members of a team may be much better at running a meeting than others. Team members should understand that the organization invites all members to practice this skill, just as if they were practicing a new software. This small act will help team members to encourage each other to host better, wiser, more cohesive meetings and to articulate why meetings succeed or fail.

ACTIVE LISTENING

When active listening becomes an integral part of meetings, it reaps myriad benefits. Active listening breeds greater understanding, improved relationships and team dynamics, and better work-product outcomes. It also ignites a curiosity that can have crossover impacts on creative thinking and interpersonal communication. Contemplative leaders can model and teach active listening to team members by focusing on three elements, known as the Three A's of Active Listening:

Attention: Listening requires deliberate, sustained attention. As someone is speaking, the active listener focuses on the words and takes time to evaluate and analyze what the speaker is saying. Mini-reflections throughout the listening session help cement core ideas in the listener's mind.

Attitude: Active listening requires an open mind and a positive attitude towards the process of listening itself. This is especially important if the subject matter is heated or tense. If the listener has made up their mind before hearing any new information, they will simply listen for bits that are in line with their pre-existing belief and ignore the other information.

Adjustment: Active listening means letting go of preconceptions about where a conversation will go and adjusting to the possibility that new, unforeseen ideas may emerge. This is not about relinquishing order but rather about allowing new ideas to arrive at the table.

PURPOSEFUL PAUSES

Leaders can implement purposeful pauses to increase self-awareness in their organization. At its core, a purposeful pause is a short meditation taken whenever the mind is overwhelmed or unfocused. Contemplative leaders can invite team members to pause prior to the start of an intense work session. The leader can be intentional about communicating their need to take a purposeful pause anytime in the course of the business day, further modeling the practice and pushing it towards becoming a regular habit among team members. Anytime a person needs a small break to regain their composure or focus, they can take a purposeful pause by:

- Intentionally stopping whatever activity they are currently doing
- Taking 3-5 minutes to sit quietly and breathe, take a short walk around the campus, go grab a refreshment, or do a stretching routine

Regular practice of purposeful pauses increases self-awareness, emotional regulation, present-state awareness, and more. The more we listen to ourselves and recognize our need to recenter ourselves, the more easily we can regroup and get back to being productive and content.

ENGAGEMENT

When people are not engaged in their professional work, they can easily become unhappy and unfulfilled. Disgruntled, they eventually leave. A culture that is contemplative actively encourages engagement among employees through direct policies and, indirectly, by aligning workflows to organizational values. Leaders may encourage open communication and inquiry about goals, plans, and desires. They may encourage team members to try new things, seek professional development opportunities, and take on additional responsibilities.

More formally, contemplative cultures can enact policies related to engagement and job satisfaction. "Job crafting," for example, is a practice that refers to an employee's ability to customize their role within an organization to maximize their strengths, interests, and goals. By creating policies that encourage this kind of plasticity, leaders can help their team bring their best, authentic selves to the work each and every day. The result is decreased turnover and increased happiness in the workplace, which of course improves bottom-line results for the organization. Often, these changes are so subtle that leadership might not even notice them. They are extremely meaningful, however, to the person being given the autonomy to craft their position to be more aligned with their authentic selves.

Flexible work schedules are another policy change that contemplative cultures can incorporate to improve employee engagement and well-being. Giving some freedom to choose the hours in which a team member works improves job satisfaction and performance. It also encourages employees to manage their time—a valuable and empowering skill in any setting. With the pandemic, remote work has become increasingly embraced, and countless organizations are realizing the power it can have in terms of productivity, retention, and engagement. Mindful leaders should be open to providing these simple, yet powerful, means to boost engagement.

MENTORSHIP

Mentorship provides both the mentor and the mentee with endless and continual opportunities to develop the emergent qualities of contemplative leadership. Within the context of fostering a more contemplative workplace, mentorship has a rightful place. Ongoing interactions between mentor and mentee can help develop empathy, present-state awareness, open mindedness, and more, and organizations that wish to intentionally move to a more contemplative culture can work to formalize a mentorship program.

Now, it is not uncommon to find a good deal of resistance to formal mentorship programs because participants sometimes feel they are being forced to take part or they lack discretion to choose their partner. Contemplative mentorship, however, can allow participants to understand these partnerships more richly. Mentor and mentee can work together through a shared practice of inner reflection that can lead to striking discoveries. In doing so, they may very well uncover one of life's cheekiest tricks: that the mentee has just as much to teach the mentor as the mentor has to teach the mentee. It is at that point that these partnerships can truly become elucidating—and great fun.

The Society for Human Resource Management, or SHRM, is an organizational and employee development organization that provides tips for creating a mentorship program. They recommend the following:

- Ensure the program is fully supported by leadership with an allocated budget
- Assign a paid administrator who leads and supports the program

- Match mentors and mentees on data instead of choosing pairs at random
- Plan purposeful group activities and experiences for training, relationship building, and networking
- Establish goals for the program overall and for mentor partnerships that can later be measured for effectiveness

Formal mentorship programs can create lasting impacts on the participating individuals, improve intra-organizational respect, boost morale, broaden skill sharing, and create many more long-term positive outcomes for the organization. The contemplative leader needs to ensure that any formalized mentoring program is designed intentionally, with thought and care for the individuals who participate.

AN INVITATION TO PRACTICE

For this exercise, you'll just need about 20 minutes. You can take notes here or in your own journal. Grab a pen, and find a comfortable place to sit that is free from distractions. Take a few moments to become relaxed and still before journaling.

What were the qualities that most resonated with you in this chapter? Consider for a moment what a contemplative or more reflective work culture may look like within your team or your organization. What qualities would you like to see demonstrated in your team?

Please take a few moments to imagine how these qualities may benefit team dynamics and improve the overall process.

Consider taking these next steps:

- If you have not already done so, speak with your team about what qualities are important to them and set an intention for supporting each other. These could in clude better work/life balance, stress reduction, mindful meetings, or whatever they feel would be most valuable. or whatever they feel would be most valuable.
- What action can you take that would help to create a collaborative workplace and build a sense of community within your team?
- Consider finding a space in your office that can be designated as a quiet room. This space can be used for meditation, silence, naps to replenish energy, etc.
- In what ways can you begin to inspire and nurture members of your team to develop practices that encourage reflection?

Slowly begin to incorporate some of these practices in your workplace. Some changes can happen more quickly, while others may be more systemic and may take a year or two. The key is to take small steps and then build on them.

CONTEMPLATIVE LEADER PROFILE

Jan Birchfield, PhD
Founder of Antara Retreat, NM
Contemplative Leadership Development Coach
Author of Silent Leaders

The contemplative practices Jan uses in her own life include:

- breath meditation
- Hanuman Chalisa devotional hymn
- chakra visualization
- Hatha Yoga
- Kriya Yoga

Jan Birchfield is founder of Antara Retreat in Taos, New Mexico, which supports leaders with strengthening the connection between inner wisdom and the actions they take in their work and the world. A family-run business, the retreat provides private and group programs for individuals who wish to incorporate contemplation into their lives or their work. It provides them with the tools and practices to move through transitions with greater insight and clarity and to increase creativity.

I reached out to Jan to learn more about her work, and she shared with me how it weaves together leadership, psychology, spirituality, shamanism, and contemplative practice. She talked about her deep passion for working with leaders who wish to increase their emotional and intuitive intelligence. She is passionate about supporting the transformation of leaders by helping them cultivate a stronger connection to inner-wisdom, which she believes is "the true source of leadership."

A long-time practitioner of meditation, Jan recognized that the leaders she was coaching yearned for deeper contemplation. Many struggled with work-life balance and were feeling distressed by the fast-paced environments in which they worked. She sensed they needed to slow down on the inside. In her desire to serve her clients more deeply, Jan felt pulled to move her family to Taos, New Mexico where she founded Antara Retreat.

Early in her career, Jan co-founded the Center for Advanced Emotional Intelligence (AEI), where she served as senior partner for eleven years. In this role, she consulted with leading companies around the country such as Campbell Soup Company, Novartis, Bristol Myers Squibb, and many others.

Jan explained to me that many leaders assume that stress is an unavoidable price one must pay in a global economy. She encourages leaders to utilize the relentless pace of their lives as a motivation for finding a deeper calm within. Through consistent practice, she believes this inspires creativity, innovation, and an expansion of one's vision.

When I asked what she would say to busy leaders who believe they do not have time for practice, she agreed that many people feel stretched to the limit and recommended they start with five minutes of stillness, removing distractions so they can be present and show up more fully. As a culture, we have a contracted sense of time, she said. We feel a sense of hurriedness, and we are extremely time-conscious. By taking brief moments of stillness, we are able to begin to access present-state awareness.

Jan talked about wanting to work with leaders who are unafraid to have these conversations and do not view discussions about contemplation as being taboo. She invites leaders "to come out of the closet," "to inquire," and "to listen to their intuition and deeper knowing."

"The intuitive mind is a sacred gift and the rational mind is a faithful servant. We have created society that honors the servant and has forgotten the gift. – Albert Einstein

CHAPTER 5

Leading with Intuition and Wisdom

In my 20 years of leadership coaching, I have yet to meet a leader who is not intuitive. What I have noticed, however, is that most of us are moving so quickly that we are not accessing the powerful internal guidance that is available to us. In today's fast-paced culture, many of us are simply overwhelmed by the sheer velocity of mental chatter. This cacophony of inner noise drowns our most valuable resource: the small voice within us that is our intuition.

And yet right now, during this time of uncertainty, rapid change, and disruption on our planet, we need intuitive leadership more than ever. As leaders, we cannot solely rely on our cognitive abilities and logic to guide our decisions and set the course for our teams and organizations. What we need is an awakening of intuition and inner wisdom. Today's leaders require intuitive intelligence to guide us not only through times of disruption and uncertainty but to lead us towards the *emergent future*.

In my practice, the majority of leaders I am currently coaching are those who have a felt sense that something is emerging. They are expressing a desire, and even a need, to lead with more thoughtfulness, intentionality, and authenticity. Deep down, they know that they must lead differently, from a place of insight and wisdom, but they are unsure where to begin. Jan Birchfield, profiled in my last chapter, writes, "Leadership, at its highest, emanates from the cultivation of inner wisdom, which is its true source." In order for leaders to access this inner wisdom, inner work is needed. She goes on to say:

> To more consistently access wisdom, three significant pieces of inner work are necessary: stabilizing our relationship to the present moment; developing a state of mind that is both relaxed and alert; and working through the aspects of our identity that are in the way. This strengthens our access to emotional and intuitive intelligence and helps us identify our blind spots, creating a strong and integrated character. And nothing is more important to leadership excellence than our personal integrity. We don't "create" wisdom. Instead, we uncover it. At the heart of the inner journey is the return to this creative stream.[10]

RESEARCH ON INTUITION

Studies show there is an intuitive part of the brain that knows what is "right" for us long before the analytical part does. For leaders, intuition is invaluable. This "gut" feeling, or inner voice, can

[10]Contemplative Leadership Development, "What Is Contemplative Leadership?" https://contemplativeld.com/whatiscontemplativeleadership, (accessed 15 May 2022). Valerie Van Mulukom, "The Science Behind Going With Your Instincts," World Economic Forum, 2018. https://www.weforum.org/agenda/2018/05/is-it-rational-to-trust-your-gut-feelings-a-neuroscientist-explains, (accessed May 15, 2022).

guide us through the noise and chaos of our lives. When we are able to successfully access it, it can help us navigate stress so we are not pulled left and right by conflicting impulses or influences.

Indeed, our new understanding of the complexities of the cognitive process allows us to see that emotions are not unintelligent responses that always need to be ignored or even corrected by rational faculties. They are, in fact, appraisals of what you have just experienced or thought. In this sense, they are a form of information processing. Research suggests that the brain is a large predictive machine, constantly comparing incoming sensory information and current experiences against stored knowledge and memories of previous experiences, and predicting what will come next.

The "predictive processing framework" as researchers call it, ensures that the brain is always prepared to deal with the current situation as optimally as possible. When a mismatch occurs and we encounter something that was not predicted, our brains update their cognitive models subconsciously—and seamlessly.

All this sheds an interesting light on the history of science. Since the 18th century's Age of Reason, mainstream thinkers have painted emotional thinking as biased and psychologically perturbed. To be modern is to be scientifically rigorous, they insist, and anything that can be punctured by scientific scrutiny is inherently flawed. Yet now, in this more recent work on the science of emotions, we see the possibility of science "confirming" the intuitive spectra of our brains. It begs the question: what else is scientific "rigor" ignoring simply because it can't see what dwells in its own blind spots?

I'll save that question for another time and say simply that our fast-paced, high-tech, 21st-century lives are giving us an opportunity to marry intellect with intuition, reason with wisdom. For the first time in centuries, we may finally be living in a time where we do not need to force ourselves to choose one over the other. While life may seem more chaotic than ever, it may in fact be a time for us, as humans, to bring forth our greatest synthesis yet.

Intuition, the powerful reserve that exists within all of us, is infinite in its size and scope. Stare for a few minutes at the way a bee homes its way to a flower, and the way the flower homes its way to the bee, and you'll see that life is more than mere cellular activity; it is an intuition, an energy, a movement. That power exists in each and every one of us. It is, in fact, the driving force that unites all life. Through it, our creativity, our innovation, and our wisdom are born. We are on this earth to intuit!

AN INVITATION TO PRACTICE

By adopting a consistent practice of stillness, you can begin to turn up the volume on the trustworthy inner voice known as intuition. Nurturing this voice requires regular practice and a new way of listening. With the busyness of our daily lives, we are not acquainted with our inner voice, and quieting the mind gives us space to listen to the wisdom it is trying to tell us.

For this exercise, you'll just need 10 to 15 minutes. You can use the notes pages here or in your own journal. Grab a pen, and find a comfortable place to sit that is free from distractions. Take a few moments to become relaxed and still. We'll continue using the 4 – 7 – 8 breathing pattern to help you quiet your mind and move into a state of deeper relaxation.

For this exercise, you'll just need 10 to 15 minutes. You can use the notes pages here or your own journal. Grab a pen, and find a comfortable place to sit that is free from distractions. Take a few moments to become relaxed and still. We'll continue using the 4 – 7 – 8 breathing pattern to help you quiet your mind and move into a state of deeper relaxation.

LET'S BEGIN.

Empty your lungs of air.
Breathe in through your nose for a count of 4 seconds.
Hold your breath for a count of 7 seconds.
Exhale on a count of 8 – when exhaling, do so audibly and with some force.
Repeat this exercise 4 times (if you feel comfortable, gently close your eyes).

In this state of relaxation and openness, I invite you to reflect on the following for your journal entry.

1. Recall a time when you had a gut sense about something but for whatever reason, you second-guessed yourself. How did that experience feel?
2. If you were to fully trust yourself with a decision, how would that look? How would it feel?
3. What are 3 to 5 ideas that you've been feeling nudged to do? How would taking these actions benefit you or your team?

If you sense an urge to keep writing, please give yourself time and space to write down any other thoughts or ideas that are coming up for you.

"Your vision will become clear only when you look into your heart. Who looks outside, dreams. Who looks inside, awakens." – Carl Jung

CHAPTER 6

Visioning for Contemplative Leadership

A practice I use in my consultancy to help leaders and teams access their intuition is a guided practice called visioning. The practice known as The Life Visioning Process™ was developed by Dr. Michael Beckwith, beloved spiritual leader and founder of the Agape International Spiritual Center in Los Angeles. The visioning process is applicable to all aspects of life—whether personal, spiritual, professional, or relational. This process has been an important part of my own contemplative practice for many years, and I have used it to find clarity in my life's purpose. I relied on this process throughout my doctoral program, and it has provided insights on how to approach my projects, including how to approach this book.

I have adapted Dr. Beckwith's visioning practice to my work with senior leaders and teams, and I have found the process to be extremely beneficial in helping organizations navigate uncertainty and change. His teachings center around making spirituality more practical in our everyday lives. Visioning is an intuitive process for opening and becoming more aware of what is wanting to emerge in our lives and organizations. More specifically, the process wants to turn our attention inward so we can become open and available to an infinite field of awareness—a field that is only accessible through our intuition or higher self.

In a state of inquiry, we open ourselves to receive any messages seeking to emerge from this intuitive inner voice, also referred to as Divine, Source, The Universe, Spirit, God, and more. I believe this inner voice can be called anything you wish. The key is to gain access to all that it is communicating to you.

Not to be confused with visualization, visioning is a process connected to your higher consciousness, whereas visualizing is a mental process, controlled by the conscious mind. In the mental process of visualization, you control what you see and are limited by your deeply ingrained, unconscious thought patterns. Visioning, conversely, is about letting go of control and allowing something previously unknown to emerge. Visualization works from the "outside-in," while visioning works from the "inside-out."

Both practices are very helpful, but they serve different purposes. Visualization creates a mental picture of where you would like to be, while visioning invites a picture or idea to emerge from a place of stillness and silence. The answers being sought will not be created from you, but rather, arrive through you.

In order for leaders to lead organizations beyond their present realities, they need a new vision for the future. It is necessary, then, to find a higher vision and an expanded reality that can transcend the familiar. Sohail Inayatullah, a global leader in futures studies, encourages organizations to "challenge the used, or predictive future and to engage in a process of co-creating alternative futures."[12] Engaging in practices such as visioning helps organizations make meaningful, long-lasting changes.

Over the past two years, the majority of the visioning sessions I've facilitated have focused on creating equitable and inclusive workplaces. Many organizations believe that equity is a matter of strategic planning. While strategic planning serves an important function to any organization, it often falls short of creating lasting, organic change.

The visioning process, on the other hand, can help organizations overcome stale, and even debilitating, patterns. By encouraging organizational leaders to begin this process with visioning, I watch how everyone involved is able to develop a plan that is more authentic and longer-lasting. Visioning allows workers to shine a light on the truths they already know in their hearts, instead of forcing an unwanted structure upon them.

One of my clients, a senior leader who wanted to create a more equitable and inclusive work culture, has used a visioning practice to great success. Rather than take a compliance-driven approach, he was genuinely interested in taking himself and his company through a process of change and transformation. Over the course of several days, I guided him and his leadership team through this reflective visioning process, which resulted in the creation of a shared vision for inclusion.

THE VISIONING PROCESS I USE

I use the following exercise in my contemplative leadership coaching, and I encourage you to try it for yourself and even with your team.

For the first 10 minutes of the session, I guide leaders and their teams through a relaxation exercise so they are open and receptive. This exercise is intended to get people out of their heads and into their hearts.

Next, I pose a series of questions to the group aimed at uncovering not just the immediate goals for leadership, the team, or the organization as a whole but the truest shared vision for the organization's future. This is broader, big picture thinking that is intended to be in service of achieving the highest potential of the organization.

- What is our highest vision for the future of the organization?
- What are the barriers to change?
- What resources are needed to lead us towards our vision?
- What structures and systems need to be changed?
- How will change or progress be measured?
- What do we already have that should be embraced and further cultivated?
- What must we let go of to clear the way forward?
- What opportunities can be created in service of the future organization?

As these questions are posed, participants are invited to be quiet and still while responses arrive from within. The responses will naturally vary from person to person. Sometimes words, phrases, images, or even colors arise. Other times, full sentences or statements may come through.

The idea is for the participants to serve as receptacles, receiving the messages that are brought forth without judgment or discrimination. In other words, there are no right or wrong answers. Whatever emerges can be viewed as a "download" of sorts from the subconscious mind to the conscious one.

Those engaging in this inquiry may choose to take notes as these thoughts, ideas, or answers come to them, and time will be afforded following each question for this purpose. Upon completion of the inquiry phase of the process, the group will share their received thoughts, which will be compiled and organized for the next steps.

While visioning opens the door to a new path forward, the exercise will not bear future fruit unless leadership uses the session to change policy, practices, and mindsets within the organization. This is where, at last, strategic planning comes to play a part. After all, a shared vision is useless without an actionable plan for meaningful change.

AN INVITATION TO PRACTICE

For this exercise, you'll want to give yourself 20 to 30 minutes. You can use the notes pages here or in your own journal. Grab a pen, and find a comfortable place to sit that is free from distractions. Take a few moments to become relaxed and still. We'll continue using the 4 - 7 - 8 breathing pattern to help you quiet your mind and move into a state of deeper relaxation.

LET'S BEGIN.

Empty your lungs of air.
Breathe in through your nose for a count of 4 seconds.
Hold your breath for a count of 7 seconds.
Exhale on a count of 8 – when exhaling, do so audibly and with some force.
Repeat this exercise 4 times (if you feel comfortable, gently close your eyes).

In a relaxed and meditative state, read the questions below. After each question, the answers may come through as images, ideas, words, symbols, etc. It's okay if you do not receive an answer right away; it may come spontaneously while you are showering, preparing for your daily cooking, or perhaps while driving.

The key is to remain open.

- – What is seeking to emerge in your leadership?
- – What is your highest vision of leadership?
- – What kind of leader wants to emerge through you?
- – What qualities do you need to release and let go of?
- – What qualities, gifts, and talents are currently serving your leadership?

Continue journaling if you feel an impulse to do so. Once you feel complete, remain still for a few moments in an atmosphere of gratitude. In addition to visioning for your highest expression of leadership, you can also use this practice to vision for anything that needs clarity in your life.

CONTEMPLATIVE LEADER PROFILE

David W. Robinson-Morris, PhD
Executive Director of Center for Contemplative Mind in Society
(CMind)
Educator & Human Rights Activist

The contemplative practices David uses in her own life include:

- Lectio Divina (Divine Reading)
- engaged Buddhism
- walking meditation

David Robinson-Morris currently serves as the Executive Director at The Center for Contemplative Mind in Society (CMind), located in western Massachusetts. A global community of practitioners, CMind is committed to the development of racial, social, economic and environmental justice, and helping to advance human flourishing. In addition, David is the founder of REImaginelution, a strategic consulting firm that helps organizations to reimagine diversity, equity, and inclusion for collective healing.

I was excited about the opportunity to meet David and found his work to be extremely inspiring. David shared with me that his work is inspired by Ubuntu—a South African philosophical concept of shared humanity. Ubuntu, coupled with engaged Buddhism, informs his ongoing understanding of our shared and collective humanity. As an executive director, entrepreneur, educator, and social rights activist, David's contemplative practices extend to all facets of his work. He spoke of embodying the practices so that the qualities radiate to those he serves. Fundamentally, he believes leaders can "become the way" for organizational transformation. This means committing deeply to "walking the talk." He acknowledges that this is not easy!

David also views his daily practices as a form of protest and of speaking up against injustices. His practice helps him engage in deep dialogue about racial, gender, and health equity with greater compassion. He explained that we are all one part of a whole—and how WE are more important than I. He is a believer in communalism and consensus building, and spoke about transcending the ego to care more deeply for the ecology of the whole.

When talking about the drastic changes we are experiencing as a society, he stated the importance of disrupting the vast injustice we are seeing. Disruption for transformation is the best disruption of all.

When I asked David about his vision for the future of contemplative leadership, he said he imagines the qualities of collaboration, community, joy, and generosity of spirit.

The primary spiritual question that drives David's work centers on what it means to be a human being. This question, and its exploration, informs how he approaches his leadership, management, teaching, and community involvement. His reflective practices support him in finding home within himself.

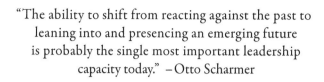

"The ability to shift from reacting against the past to leaning into and presencing an emerging future is probably the single most important leadership capacity today." – Otto Scharmer

CHAPTER 7

Reimagining the Future of Leadership

The world as we once knew it no longer exists, and leadership is changing before our eyes. One thing is certain: we are living in a different world than we did just a few short years ago, and it is unlikely that the world will go back to the way it was. Globalization, climate change, artificial intelligence, remote work—all are changing the human experience, and quickly. Otto Scharmer, MIT professor and author of Theory U, describes how the present moment requires a wholly different approach than anything we could have imagined:

> "The crisis of our time isn't just a crisis of a single leader, organization, country, or conflict. The crisis of our time reveals the dying of an old social structure and way of thinking, an old way of institutionalizing and enacting collective social forms."

No MBA or executive training could have prepared us for the degree of disruption and unpredictability we face, and these times require very different leadership capabilities if we are to steer our organizations and people towards a future we want.

In fact, the pace of change will only accelerate, regardless of size or the type of business or organization. Conventional styles of leadership and outdated strategies are not sustainable in today's reality, and we need a new, adaptive, and mindful or contemplative kind of leadership.

To reimagine this new kind of leadership, we need to step outside our present paradigm. We must find the courage to embrace disruption and uncertainty from a place of wisdom and poise. Leading through this ambiguity calls for an expanded vision and higher thinking. Such a potent, transformative moment in history presents us with a great potential for transformation.

As we chart this unknown future, we need leaders who can help our society feel confident, unafraid, diplomatic, loving, and innovative. Jacob Morgan, author of The Future Leader, states that change is a constant in the 21st century. Whether through the effects of globalization, climate change, artificial intelligence, remote work, limited resources, damaged supply chains, or other destabilization, change is happening to all of us, and it's happening so quickly. Every business and organization, regardless of its size, is quaking.

In these unprecedented times, we need leaders who:

1. can juggle the world's mounting contradictions. Today's world is full of strange dualities, and it is important that we accept these rather than trying to privilege one over the other.

For example, at the same time that human cultures are more connected than ever, they are also more fractured than ever. As F. Scott Fitzgerald wrote, we need leaders who can, "hold two (or even more) opposing ideas in mind at the same time and still retain the ability to function," for "it is through the exploration of uncertainty that we arrive at better outcomes."

2. believe in creating a long-term vision rather than merely short-term gains.

3. can break free from a blind reliance on data-driven predictions to focus, instead, on intuitive foresight.

4. can find the courage to let go of the broken systems that are failing our citizens and can work to envision a better path forward.

5. can serve as models for today by leading with both the courage and the humility that dwells within a contemplative heart.

6. have let go of the unhealthy way of sidelining health and well-being in favor of productivity. Our new leaders prioritize the well-being of themselves, their famlies, and their colleagues. They willingly challenge the status quo of individuals running on a treadmill and burning themselves out. They understand that, in order to survive, leaders and their respective organizations require resilience, calmness, and compassion.

7. exhibit understanding, compassion, and empathy for each other as human beings. As we reimagine leadership, let us consider a new arsenal of skills and values the future resilient leader will need, especially during times of crisis and uncertainty.

8. have addressed the battlefield of the mind and use contemplative practice to respond to the constant barrage of information and constant change. This practice gives them a measured calm, clarity, and focus, instead of agitation, confusion, and fear.

9. create a safe, supportive, and productive environment for their teams and staff no matter what arises in the world.

10. reshape the future today by using intuition and imagination. They look inside themselves to appreciate and understand the magnificent potential therein. By contemplating within, they see they have everything they need to move forward, and they understand things will be as they should be in the end. This attitude colors and influences how they see the world around them, from the smallest to the largest tasks.

11. use their self-awareness, calmness, and confidence to reshape their workplaces and teams, realizing the answers to questions exist only when we remain quiet and listen.

12. willingly employ transparency. Leaders are being asked to lead during a new era of corporate and personal responsibility. Successful leaders must apply a rigorous transparency to their actions. This openness will signal their leadership style and will make a cultural difference to their organization immediately. In addition to this, however, leaders must take responsibility for their decisions in our increasingly complex world.

13. see how today's choices will impact the future masses and the planet. Contemplative leaders' understanding of the complexity of our world defines the most critical quality of resilient

leaders today: they create strategies that sustain their organizations for the remainder of the 21st Century and beyond.

When empowered by strategic foresight, contemplative leaders forecast scenarios of the future more insightfully than others because their minds are more inclined towards higher thinking and intuition. They are not fortune-tellers who always anticipate specific disruptions, but they do see conflicts coming long before those without expanded consciousness. They innovate and navigate through change—disruptive or otherwise.

If you take time to get to know your own voice within you, you will discover that the future is not asking you to retreat. Instead, it is inviting you to embark on a new journey.

MOVING THROUGH RESISTANCE

Whenever we are presented with a new path, we find ourselves engaging with a rush of unbridled emotion. Feelings of excitement, ambition, regret, and disappointment swirl together, often appearing muddy and confusing. As you take further steps down this leadership path, I encourage you to keep a journal to be mindful of how these emotions roll in and out of your life.

Resistance may tell us we do not need to change, or we are changing too fast. When your brain presents you with resistance, it does so in strange ways. It can make you paranoid or irritable or emotional in ways that have almost nothing to do with the reality of your situation. When these emotions present themselves, they are usually so out of character that the moments act as signposts on your journey. They say, "There is resistance here." And that is how you know that you are going to need to dig around in that spot a little more. You're going to have to figure out what is blocking your journey. What is this stalled moment waiting to teach you?

These mucky, difficult areas are the most potent, most "nutrient-rich" areas of your growth. When you encounter them, it is important not to see them as signs of discouragement but rather as very much the opposite. They are signs that your work is working—that you are changing, going deeper and deeper into your truth.

I like to use the Buddhist symbol of the lotus flower when talking about points of resistance. The lotus, one of the most beautiful flowers on earth, needs the rich mud in order to thrive. From the ugliest source, it produces a breathtaking flower. That flower is like our spiritual lives: born from mud and reborn as beauty.

Despite the urgent pull to create organizational change, many leaders resist. My hope is that an engagement with contemplative leadership can help them, and their organizations, ease naturally into a transformative process that moves with their innermost voice rather than against it.

Be kind to yourself, and to others, and remember: when you feel lost, turn within. Your Self is waiting for you.

QUESTIONS FOR REFLECTION

1. If you consider the future of your own leadership, what qualities do you believe are needed to guide your team or organizations?

2. If you were to predict another pandemic, another crisis, or racial reckoning, how would you respond? What resources would you use to support you?

3. How do you engage your team to collectively respond to the disruptive challenges of our time?

4. In what ways does your resistance show up? Does it appear during moments when you feel fear, doubt, or a need to control an outcome?

Reimagining invites us to connect with our highest future possibility — to create a vision for ourselves, our teams, and our organization and bring it into the present. Reimagining asks us to release an old paradigm and open ourselves up to something completely different.

HOW CONTEMPLATIVE PRACTICES HELP

When faced with a barrage of often-conflicting information and fresh challenges, the mind must sort things and see clearly. Contemplative practice enables leaders to respond to constant change from a place of measured calm, clarity, and focus, instead of agitation, confusion, and fear.

As a contemplative practitioner, I am deeply committed to re-imagining the future of leadership, and extending an invitation to contemplative leadership to all who lead and serve. Contemplative leadership offers a path for leading mindfully through crisis and uncertainty.

I am honored to have shared this book with you. This writing experience has been a transformative journey for me, and I hope the reading experience will be a transformative journey for you!

CONTINUE YOUR JOURNEY WITH THESE RESOURCES

RETREATS

1. **1440 Multiversity**
   https://www.1440.org/

2. **Copper Beech Institute**
   https://www.copperbeechinstitute.org/

3. **Esalen**
   https://www.esalen.org/

4. **Kripalu Center for Yoga and Health Studies**
   https://kripalu.org/

5. **Omega**
   https://www.eomega.org/

6. **Rythmia Life Advancement Center**
   https://www.rythmialifeadvancement.com/

7. **The Path**
   https://www.thepath.com

BOOKS

From Mindfulness to Heartfulness
Stephen Murphy-Shigematsu

Presence
Peter Senge, Otto Scharmer, Joseph Jaworski & Betty Sue Flowers

Mindful Leadership
Maria Gonzalez

Silent Leaders
Jan Birchfield

The Future Leader
Jacob Morgan

The Life Visioning Process
Dr. Michael Beckwith

The Power of Full Engagement
Jim Loehr

Theory U
Otto Scharmer

ABOUT THE AUTHOR

Dr. Thulani DeMarsay is a leadership coach, organizational development consultant, and researcher deeply invested in reimagining the future of leadership. For over 20 years, she has had the privilege of working with a diverse population of leaders, including corporate executives, entrepreneurs, and professional men and women throughout New England. She helps senior leaders and teams build the inner capacity needed to guide their organizations, particularly during times of crisis, change, and uncertainty.

Thulani works closely with leaders and teams to create a contemplative practice. In addition, she facilitates workshops and retreats. She is passionate about developing innovative solutions that inspire dialogue, critical self-reflection, and individual and group transformation. She is currently researching how reflective practices such as mindfulness and meditation help reduce unconscious bias and foster inclusive workplaces.

Thulani completed her doctoral degree in Human Development from Fielding Graduate University. Her dissertation research explored the ways that contemplative practices such as mindfulness, meditation, centering prayer, and yoga foster resilience to stress and improve leadership effectiveness.